Fons&Porter
Cincinnati, Ohio

quilt lovely

15 Vibrant Projects
Using Piecing
& Appliqué

JEN KINGWELL

Contents

USING THIS BOOK--------------

 This symbol refers to crosscutting a square once on the diagonal.

 This symbol refers to crosscutting a square twice on the diagonal.

Finished block measurement refers to the size of a block in the completed quilt. Therefore, a 4" (10.2cm) finished measurement will be 4½" (11.4cm) before sewing (due to seam allowances).

Traditionally, measurements used in quilt making are Imperial and most of the equipment follows suit. In this book, you will find both Imperial and metric measurements listed. Fabric requirements given are based on 44"–wide (111.8cm–wide) fabric.

--------------------SEAM ALLOWANCES

For rotary-cut and machine-pieced projects, a ¼" (6mm) seam allowance is included in the instructions.

For hand-pieced or appliquéed projects, draw your stitching line around your template, then add your seam allowance.

Some projects in this book include both hand and machine techniques; this is stipulated on each project.

Read all instructions before beginning a project.

IMPORTANT TIPS--------------------

Press seam allowances toward the darker fabric unless it will cause excessive bulk.

Check in which direction the seams are pressed and do not allow them to become twisted when you sew blocks together.

Your needles should be changed after every eight hours of stitching.

Replace rotary blades regularly. New blades make a big difference in fabric cuts and cause less frustration.

When buying fabric and equipment, purchase the best quality you can afford.

Always remove selvedges.

chapter 1

Quilts

Patchwork of all types has been practiced for centuries. Patchwork clothing was common in the past, but the majority of the pieces that have survived are quilts or bedcovers.

These items were originally made out of necessity or economy. In the following decades, when cottons became plentiful and pretty, patchwork became more fashionable and stitching became a pastime.

Quilting has become an art form. The skills are not difficult to learn, and the satisfaction from creating something both beautiful and useful is profound.

We can now choose from thousands of lovely fabrics in exciting colors and prints. We have notions and sewing aids that would leave our forebearers speechless. The variety available to us is staggering.

I am in love with color and print. My mood is lifted when I'm surrounded by the infinite varieties of fabric. My soul is fed. I want to share this passion with all of you.

I hope you enjoy these projects and that there is something here to brighten your days and intensify your love of quilting.

This quilt can be hand- or machine-pieced and is easily adapted to any size. The project shown uses three fabrics in each block, but you can make yours more eclectic if you desire.

▼ MATERIALS & SUPPLIES

6 yds. (5.5m) total fabric in a variety of patterns, colors, solids and tone-on-tones (fat sixteenths work well)

4½ yds. (4.1m) fabric for backing

⅝ yd. (57.2cm) fabric for binding

2⅛ yds. (2m) square of batting

Template plastic

Sewing machine

¼" (6mm) sewing machine foot

Matching cotton thread for sewing

Aurifil 12-weight thread for hand quilting

Rotary cutter

Cutting mat

Ruler

General sewing notions (pins, scissors, tape measure, etc.)

Templates T1, T2, T3, T4 and T4 REVERSE (on pattern sheet 1)

---------- **A NOTE ABOUT FABRIC**
Hundreds of different fabrics were used for this quilt. For each block, the T1 pieces, T3 pieces and center square (T2) were cut from the same focus fabric. The T4 pieces were cut from a different background fabric, and the remaining 4 squares (T2) were cut from a third contrast fabric.

Cutting Instructions
Finished block measures 3½" × 9⅛" (8.9cm × 23.2cm).

Make 152 blocks total.

For each block, cut:
2 from template T1 from focus fabric (304 total)

2 from template T3 from focus fabric (304 total)

2 from template T4 from background fabric (304 total)

2 from template T4 REVERSE from background fabric (304 total)

5 from template T2, 1 from focus fabric and 4 from contrast fabric (152 total from focus and 304 from contrast)

Note: Fabrics for template T2 can be rotary cut at 1¾" (4.4cm) square. For template T3, cut 1 square at 2⅛" (5.4cm) and crosscut once on the diagonal ◻.

Block Assembly
At this point, you'll have decided whether to machine piece or hand piece your quilt top. The assembly method is the same for both styles, but you need to keep your seam allowance free and unstitched at the Y seam so you can easily insert the background pieces.

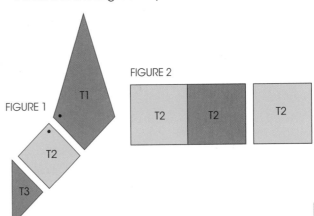

FIGURE 1

FIGURE 2

1 | Stitch a T1 shape to a square of contrast fabric (template T2), then stitch to triangle T3. Leave the seam allowance unstitched at the junctions marked by the black dots (*Figure 1*). Make 2.

2 | Stitch 3 T2 squares together (*Figure 2*).

3 | Stitch the unit together as shown in Figure 3.

4 | Insert the background T4 and T4 REVERSE pieces as shown in Figure 4. Begin stitching at the black dot (backstitch to secure). Leaving the seam allowance free, stitch to the outer edge of the block, then repeat and stitch up to the end of the block.

Quilt Assembly

5 | Lay your blocks out to get an even distribution of color and pattern, then stitch them together in horizontal rows. You will need to make 8 rows with 19 blocks in each (see the assembly diagram).

6 | Join the rows with long, horizontal seams. For each row, press the seam allowance in alternating directions.

7 | Your quilt top is now complete. Layer with batting, baste and prepare to quilt.

FIGURE 3

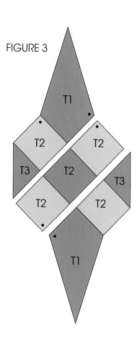

FIGURE 4

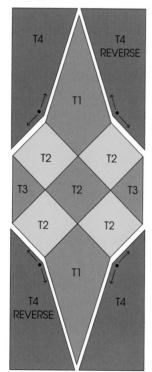

Assembly Diagram

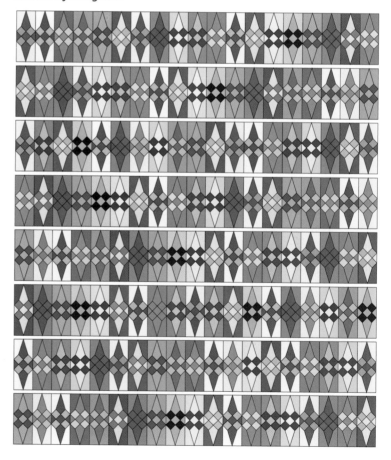

Quilting

8 | Quilt as desired. I hand quilted this project in horizontal and vertical rows through the center of the blocks. I used Aurifil 12-weight thread.

Binding

9 | Cut the binding fabric into 2½" (6.4cm) strips across the width of the fabric. Apply it to the quilt as a double binding.

▲ **Glitter Quilt,** 66½" × 73" (169cm × 185cm)

Simply Red Center

❖ Quilt measures 70" (178cm) square

This quilt is based on a small photograph I have of an antique quilt, maker unknown. The quilt was presented for appraisal at a UK quilt fair. It is made using a combination of hand appliqué and machine piecing. I love the combination of the traditional design with a primitive approach to the appliqué. I've made mine using a low-volume color palette, but it would work in a number of colors, depending on your style.

▼ MATERIALS & SUPPLIES

2¼ yds. (2.1m) background fabric for center square and outer border blocks

1⅝ yds. (1.5m) background fabric for appliqué vase border

1 fat quarter for the center appliqué

½ yd. (46cm) total of red fabrics for the Irish Chain blocks

⅓ yd. (30cm) fabric for the center of the Square in a Square blocks

½ yd. (46cm) of Round 1 fabric for the Square in a Square blocks

A variety of fat eights and fat sixteenths, including stripes and geometrics or florals for appliqué stems and flowers

¼ yd. (23cm) fabric for vase T5

⅓ yd. (30cm) fabric for vase T6

4½ yds. (4m) fabric for backing

⅝ yd. (57.2cm) fabric for binding

2¼ yds. (2.1m) square of batting

Template plastic

Sewing machine

¼" (6mm) sewing machine foot

Matching cotton thread for sewing

Perle 12-weight thread for hand quilting

Rotary cutter

Cutting mat

18½" (47cm) square ruler

24½" × 6½" (62.2cm × 16.5cm) ruler

Freezer paper

General sewing notions (pins, scissors, tape measure, etc.)

Templates T5, T6, T47, T48, T49, T50, T51, T52, T53 and Center Appliqué (on pattern sheet 2) (see appliqué layout guides on pattern sheet 1 for flower and vase arrangements)

Center Square

1 | Cut a piece of freezer paper to 18" (45.7cm) square. (If your paper is not wide enough, iron 2 strips together and overlap by 2" [5.1cm]. It will easily peel off your ironing board.)

2 | Fold the square in half, then in half again, and then fold on the diagonal (*Figure 1*).

3 | Pin the center appliqué pattern to the freezer paper and cut it out on the drawn lines (*Figure 2*).

4 | Open the freezer paper and press it shiny-side down to the fabric you wish to appliqué. Carefully cut out the design (the 1⁄8" [3.2mm] seam allowance is included in this pattern piece). Peel the freezer paper off the fabric (*Figure 3*).

5 | Cut your background fabric for the center square to 17½" (44.5cm). Lightly press the diagonal lines onto this background square. It should be easy to center the appliqué using the diagonal markings and the center junction of the pressed lines.

6 | Needle turn the appliqué in place (a 1⁄8" [3.2mm] seam allowance is included in the cut template). When finished, set it aside.

Appliqué Borders

7 | Cut 4 strips of fabric down the length of your background fabric. These will be cut at 17" × 55" (43.2cm × 139.7cm).

8 | Fold 1 strip in half. Measure across 8¾" (22.3cm) from the fold and mark (*Figure 4*).

9 | Orient your ruler with the 45° angle along the edge of the fabric and line up the straight edge of your ruler so it intersects the 8¾" (22.3cm) mark (*Figure 5*).

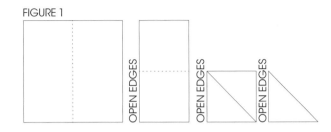

FIGURE 1

OPEN EDGES   OPEN EDGES   OPEN EDGES

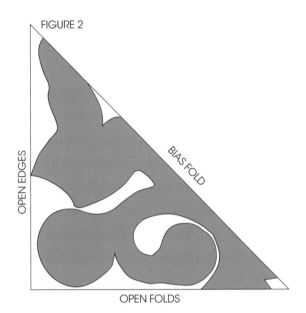

FIGURE 2

OPEN EDGES

BIAS FOLD

OPEN FOLDS

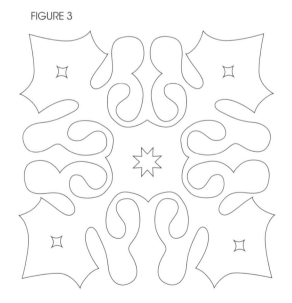

FIGURE 3

10 | Cut your fabric to create a 45° angle. This angle will create a mitered corner when you stitch your borders together.

11 | Repeat steps 8–11 with the remaining 3 border strips.

Note: *The appliqué on these borders is quite primitive, so you don't need to mark your background at all. Taking the time to center the vases, however, will help with the overall balance of the quilt design.*

12 | Cut 4 of the T5 vase template, as well as enough leaves and flowers to make 4 of the vase arrangement shown in the Simply Red Center 1 appliqué layout on pattern sheet 1.

13 | Following the Figure 6 diagram, center the T5 vase pieces on the border with the lower stitched edges ¾" (1.9cm) from the edge of the fabric. Appliqué the lower two-thirds of the vase in place, leaving the top open. This will allow you to slip the ends of the stems beneath the vases.

14 | Make bias strips for the stems.
I used a ⅜" (9mm) Clover Bias Tape Maker and cut my fabrics at ¾" (1.9cm) wide on the bias (if you prefer, you can cut and fold your bias tape by hand).

Hint: *Make all of your bias tape at the same time, then wrap it around a plastic wrap roll or plastic water bottle and secure the ends with masking tape. This will keep your bias tape flat. I also spray starch my strips before threading them through the maker, which gives them a crisp edge and helps to keep them folded. You can also press the curves in the stems at this point if you wish.*

15 | Appliqué the stems, followed by the leaves, then the flowers. The flowers and the vase should cover the ends of the stems. Lastly, complete the appliqué on the top of the vase. Refer to the quilt appliqué layout guides on pattern sheet 1 for placement.

16 | Appliqué the 4 border panels (refer to the appliqué layouts on pattern sheet 1). When this is complete, stitch the mitered corners, remembering to leave the ¼" (6mm) seam allowance unstitched at the inner end of the seams. You will have a box with a hole in the center. Press the seams open. It's less bulky and makes the appliqué easier if the center is not added at this time.

17 | Cut 4 of the T6 vase template, as well as enough leaves and flowers to make 4 of the vase arrangement shown in the Simply Red Center 2 appliqué layout on pattern sheet 1.

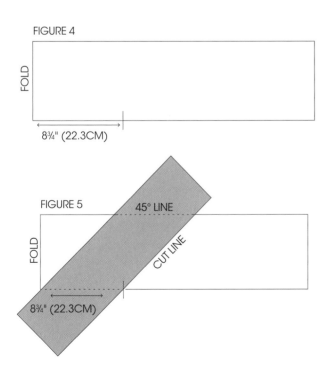

FIGURE 4

FOLD

8¾" (22.3CM)

FIGURE 5

FOLD

45° LINE

CUT LINE

8¾" (22.3CM)

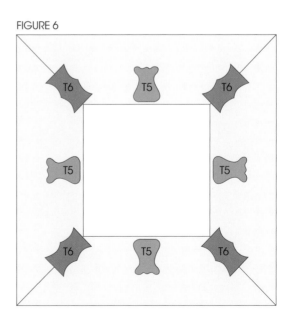

FIGURE 6

T6   T5   T6

T5   T5

T6   T5   T6

Irish Chain Block Assembly Diagram

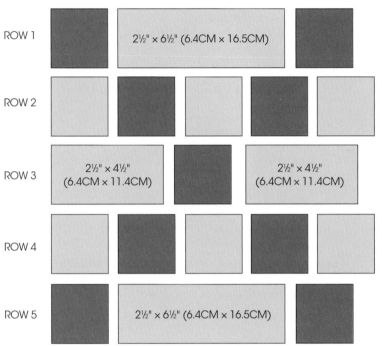

ROW 1

2½" × 6½" (6.4CM × 16.5CM)

ROW 2

ROW 3

2½" × 4½"
(6.4CM × 11.4CM)

2½" × 4½"
(6.4CM × 11.4CM)

ROW 4

ROW 5

2½" × 6½" (6.4CM × 16.5CM)

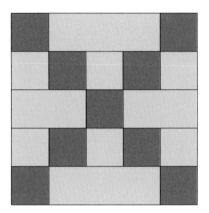

18 | Center the T6 vase pieces over the mitered seams. Following the Figure 6 diagram and the previous instructions, appliqué a vase and flowers in each of the 4 corners.

19 | Once all appliqué is complete, insert the center square. Remember to leave the seam allowance unstitched so the center will sit flat at the mitred corners.

Outer Border

This border is made of alternating Irish Chain blocks and Square in a Square blocks. A ¼" (6mm) seam allowance is included in all cutting instructions.

Irish Chain Blocks

Finished block size is 10" (25.4cm).

Make 12 blocks total.

From red fabrics, cut:
108 squares at 2½" (6.4cm) (9 squares per block)

From background fabric, cut:
72 squares at 2½" (6.4cm) (6 squares per block)

24 rectangles at 2½" × 4½" (6.4cm × 11.4cm) (2 rectangles per block)

24 rectangles at 2½" × 6½" (6.4cm × 16.5cm) (2 rectangles per block)

BLOCK ASSEMBLY

20 | Stitch the pieces together as shown in the block assembly diagram and press the seam allowance toward the darker fabric.

Square in a Square Blocks

Finished block size is 10" (25.4cm).

Make 12 blocks total.

From center square fabric, cut:
12 squares at 5½" (14cm) (1 square per block)

From Round 1 fabric, cut:
24 squares at 4⅜" (11.1cm), crosscut once on the diagonal (2 squares per block)

From background fabric, cut:
24 squares at 5⅞" (14.9cm), crosscut once on the diagonal (2 squares per block)

BLOCK ASSEMBLY

21 | Stitch the Round 1 triangles to the opposite sides of the center square (*Figure 7*). Press the seam allowance to the outside edge.

22 | Repeat with the remaining Round 1 triangles (*Figure 8*). Press.

23 | Repeat with the background triangles (*Figure 9*). Remember to press after adding the first set of triangles, then add the remaining triangles and press again.

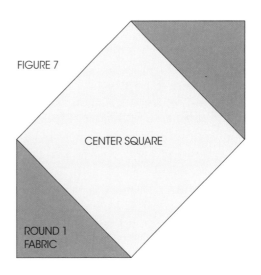

FIGURE 7

CENTER SQUARE

ROUND 1 FABRIC

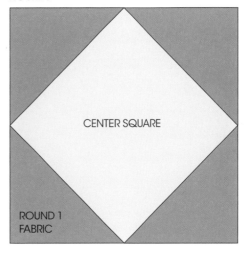

FIGURE 8

CENTER SQUARE

ROUND 1 FABRIC

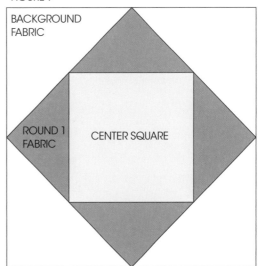

FIGURE 9

BACKGROUND FABRIC

ROUND 1 FABRIC

CENTER SQUARE

Outer Border Assembly

24 | Create 2 borders, alternating the Square in a Square blocks and the Irish Chain blocks as shown in Figure 10, then stitch these borders to each side of the quilt.

25 | Create 2 borders following the block arrangement in Figure 11, then stitch them to the top and bottom of the quilt.

Your quilt top is now complete!

Quilting

26 | Quilt as desired. I quilted this project with Perle 12-weight thread echoing the appliqué, Square in a Square and Irish Chain blocks.

Binding

27 | Cut the binding fabric into 2½" (6.4cm) strips across the width of the fabric. Apply as a double binding.

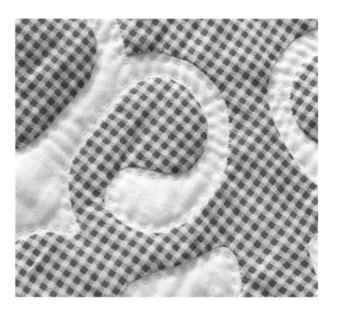

FIGURE 10

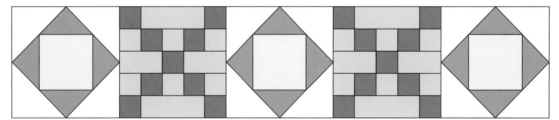

FIGURE 11

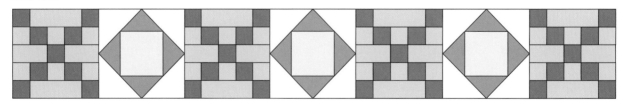

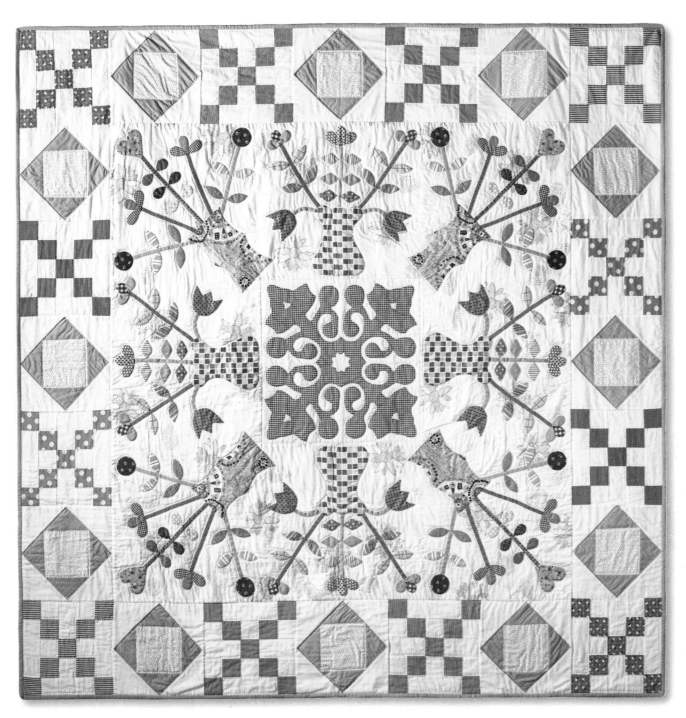

▲ **Simply Red Center,** 70" (178cm) square

Spinning Around

❖ Quilt measures 75" × 84¾" (190.5cm × 215.3cm)

This classic strippy quilt features three different pinwheels. It's simple yet effective, and it uses a riot of color. If you choose to take a more uniform or subdued approach to your palette, however, it'll still look great.

▼ MATERIALS & SUPPLIES

3⅞ yds. (3.5m) fabric total for panels and setting triangles (directional fabric will require more and will depend on the pattern repeat)

3⅓ yds. (3m) fabric total of colored fabrics for blocks in a variety of patterns, colors, solids and tone-on-tones (fat sixteenths work well)

5¼ yd. (4.8m) fabric for backing

⅔ yd. (61cm) fabric for binding

94" × 85" (2.4m × 2.2m) of batting

Sewing machine

¼" (6mm) sewing machine foot

Matching cotton thread for sewing

Perle 12-weight thread for hand quilting

Template plastic

Rotary cutter

Cutting mat

Ruler

General sewing notions (pins, scissors, tape measure, etc.)

Cutting instructions include a ¼" (6mm) seam allowance.

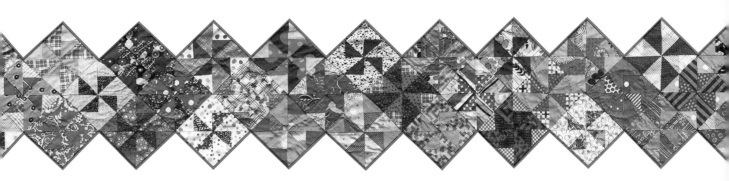

Double Pinwheel Block

Finished block measures 5¼" (13.5cm)

Make 37 blocks total.

From these cutting instructions, you will make 2 pinwheels, which are reversed.

For Combo 1, cut:
2 strips from dark fabric 8" × 2" (20.3cm × 5.1cm) (19 total)

2 strips from light fabric 8" × 2" (20.3cm × 5.1cm) (19 total)

For Combo 2, cut:
2 strips from dark fabric 8" × 2" (20.3cm × 5.1cm) (19 total)

2 strips from light fabric 8" × 2" (20.3cm × 5.1cm) (19 total)

BLOCK ASSEMBLY

1 | For each combo set, stitch the dark and light strips together in pairs along the 8" (20.3cm) sides. Press the seam allowance toward the darker fabric.

2 | Cut each strip pair into two 3½" (8.9cm) squares (*Figure 1*).

3 | Crosscut these squares once on the diagonal (*Figure 2*). It is important that you cut in this manner to create the box effect.

4 | Stitch the triangles together using 1 triangle from each combo (*Figure 3*). Make 4.

5 | Stitch these 4 units together to create your Double Pinwheel block (*Figure 4*).

6 | Repeat steps 1–5 with the remaining triangles in the reverse combination (*Figure 5*). Make 37 blocks total.

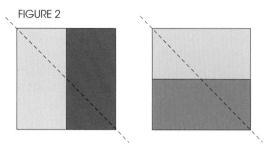
FIGURE 2

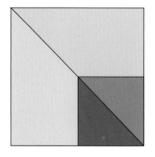
FIGURE 3

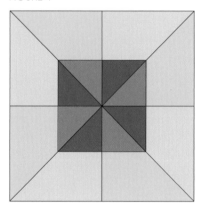
FIGURE 4

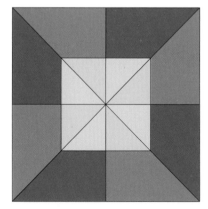
FIGURE 5

FIGURE 1

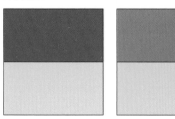

7 | Make 11 rows with 3 blocks each (*Figure 6*). Be sure to evenly distribute the colors and prints.

8 | Make 2 rows containing 2 blocks. Set aside.

Simple Pinwheel Blocks
Finished block measures 4" (10.2cm).

Make 44 blocks and 2 half blocks total.

You can make each pinwheel using as few as 2 fabrics or as many as you would like. Use 12 for a truly scrappy look. The choice is yours. I used a combination of effects in the project shown.

For each block, cut:
2 squares at 2⅞" (7.3cm) (90 total). Crosscut once on the diagonal 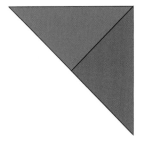.

1 square at 3¼" (8.3cm) from 2 different fabrics (90 total). Crosscut twice on the diagonal 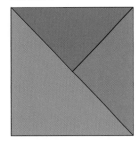.

BLOCK ASSEMBLY

9 | Take a small triangle cut from each of the 2 different fabrics and stitch them together (*Figure 7*). Make 4 total.

10 | Stitch this unit to a larger triangle to form a square (*Figure 8*). Make 4 total.

11 | Stitch 4 squares together to create your Simple Pinwheel block (*Figure 9*).
Make 44 blocks total.

12 | Using the same instructions, make 2 half blocks (*Figure 10*).

13 | Stitch the blocks together in rows of 3. Make 14 rows. Be sure to evenly distribute the colors and prints. You will have 2 full blocks and 2 half blocks remaining. These will be added later. Set them aside with the finished row for now.

FIGURE 8

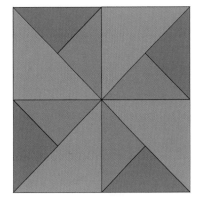

FIGURE 6

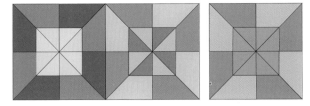

FIGURE 7

FIGURE 9

FIGURE 10

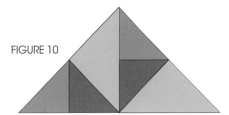

21

Firecracker Pinwheel Blocks

Finished block measures 6" (15.2cm).

Make 29 blocks and 2 half blocks total.

You can make each pinwheel using as few as 2 fabrics or as many as you would like. Use 9 for a truly scrappy look.

From colored fabrics, cut:

1 square at 4¼" (10.8cm) (30 total). Crosscut twice on the diagonal ⊠.

Repeat with 1 square of contrast fabric (30 total).

From background fabric, cut:

Cut 4 rectangles at 1⅜" × 3⅞" (3.5cm × 9.8cm) (120 total)

Cut 1 square at 4¼" (10.8cm) (30 total). Crosscut twice on the diagonal ⊠.

14 | Stack the 4 rectangles on top of each other with the wrong sides facing up. Place the 45° angle of your ruler on the lower edge of the fabric, and place the straight edge of the ruler at the corner of the rectangle (*Figure 11*). Trim and discard the small corner triangle.

BLOCK ASSEMBLY

15 | Stitch together a triangle of background fabric and a triangle of colored fabric (*Figure 12*).

16 | Stitch together a triangle of contrast fabric and a trimmed rectangle (*Figure 13*).

17 | Stitch units made in steps 15 and 16 together (*Figure 14*). Make 4 total.

18 | Stitch the 4 units together to create your Firecracker Pinwheel block (*Figure 15*). Make 29 blocks total.

19 | Using the same instructions, make 2 half blocks (*Figure 16*).

20 | Stitch the blocks together in rows of 3. Make sure to evenly distribute the colors and prints.
    Make 9 rows. You will have 2 extra blocks and 2 half blocks left over. Set these aside for now.

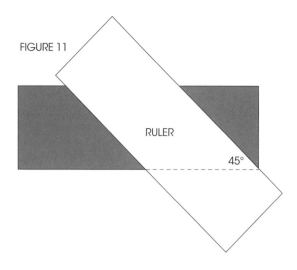

FIGURE 11

RULER

45°

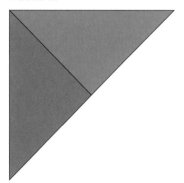

FIGURE 12

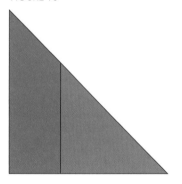

FIGURE 13

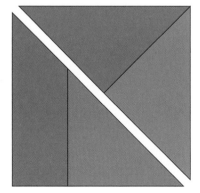

FIGURE 14

Quilt Assembly

PANEL CUTTING INSTRUCTIONS

21 | You will need to cut your long panels before you start cutting your setting triangles. Cut the fabric at 86½" (219.7cm) by at least 34" (86.4cm) wide. From this, cut 4 panels at 8½" (21.6cm) wide down the length. Set aside.

SETTING TRIANGLE INSTRUCTIONS

The triangles will fill in the spaces at the sides of the strips. If your fabric choice is not directional, you can rotary cut the squares and crosscut them twice on the diagonal. This will put your straight of grain on the outside edge, which will assist with accuracy and provide less stretch when you stitch the long panels together.

If you have chosen a directional print fabric like the stripe in the sample, you will need to make a template from one of the triangles.

Note: *You may need to adjust your fabric requirements depending on the design repeat.*

Cut strips across the width or down the length of the fabric. This will depend upon the directional design of your fabric. Mark and cut these triangles from this strip. Orient your triangles as shown in Figure 17, being careful to correctly orient your fabric pattern if it is directional.

For the Simple Pinwheels, cut:

8 squares at 6⅞" (17.5cm) and crosscut twice on the diagonal 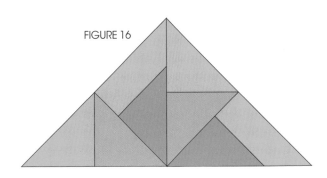.

If using a template, cut strips at 3½" (8.9cm) wide and cut 32 triangles.

For the Double Pinwheels, cut:

6 squares at 8¾" (22.2cm) and crosscut twice on the diagonal 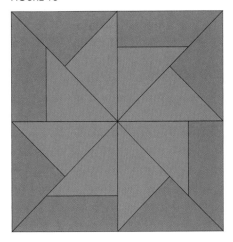.

If using a template, cut strips at 4⅜" (11.1cm) wide and cut 26 triangles.

For the Firecracker Pinwheels, cut:

6 squares at 9¾" (24.8cm) and crosscut twice on the diagonal .

If using a template, cut strips at 4⅞" (12.4cm) wide and cut 22 triangles.

FIGURE 15

FIGURE 16

FIGURE 17

PINWHEEL PANEL ASSEMBLY

22 | Take a row of pinwheels and stitch the corresponding triangle to each end (*Figure 18*).

Note: *The end of your triangle will extend past the edge of the block (*Figure 19*). This is necessary to ensure you have enough seam allowance.*

23 | Stitch the rows together to create long panels (*Figure 20*).

24 | For the top and bottom rows in the panels containing the Firecracker Pinwheels and the Simple Pinwheels, stitch 1 block to the half block (*Figure 21*).

25 | Sew setting triangles to the corners (*Figure 22*).

26 | Trim the excess from the setting triangles so they are level across the top with the edge of your half block (*Figure 23*).

Note: *For the panel of double pinwheels, your top and bottom will be little different.*

27 | Stitch the block rows together as previously instructed in steps 22–25.

The top and bottom rows consist of the previously made rows containing 2 blocks. These panels will be trimmed back across the top and bottom after calculating the length of your quilt (*Figure 24*).

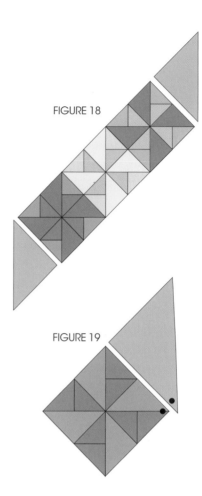

FIGURE 18

FIGURE 19

FIGURE 20

ROW ASSEMBLY

28 | Measure your panels. The Simple Pinwheel and the Firecracker panels should measure 84¾" (215cm) long.

29 | Trim the Double Pinwheel panel to match these. Remember to measure out from the center of the panel to ensure you trim the top and bottom at the same point.

30 | Trim the previously cut 8½" (21.6cm) fabric panels to the same length (84¾" [215cm]) and stitch them together. It is much easier to stitch them together if you make 2 halves and then stitch these together (refer to the assembly diagram).

31 | Your quilt top is now complete. Baste before quilting.

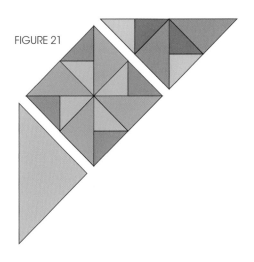

FIGURE 21

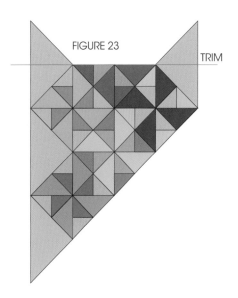

FIGURE 23

TRIM

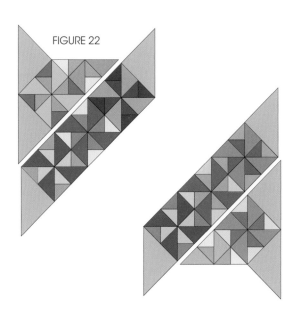

FIGURE 22

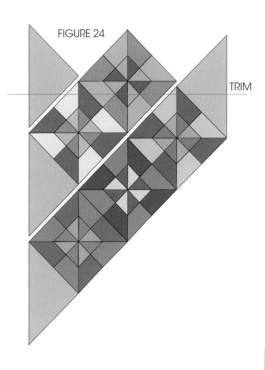

FIGURE 24

TRIM

Quilting

32 | Quilt as desired. This project was hand quilted with Perle 12-weight thread. Straight lines were quilted 1½" (3.8cm) apart down the fabric panels and random interlocking circles were quilted down the pinwheel panels.

Binding

33 | Cut 2½" (6.4cm) strips across the width of the fabric. Apply as a double binding.

Assembly Diagram

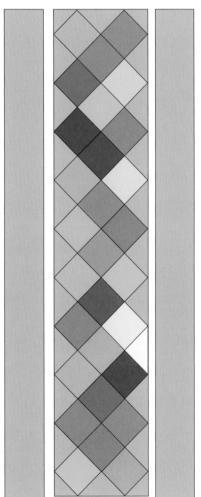
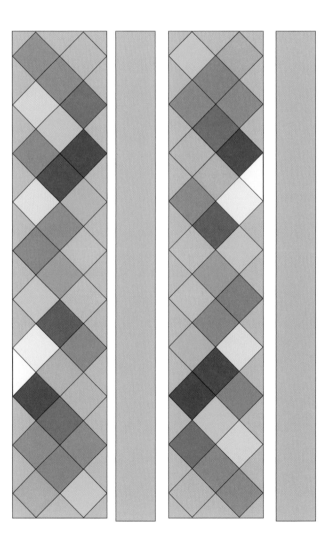

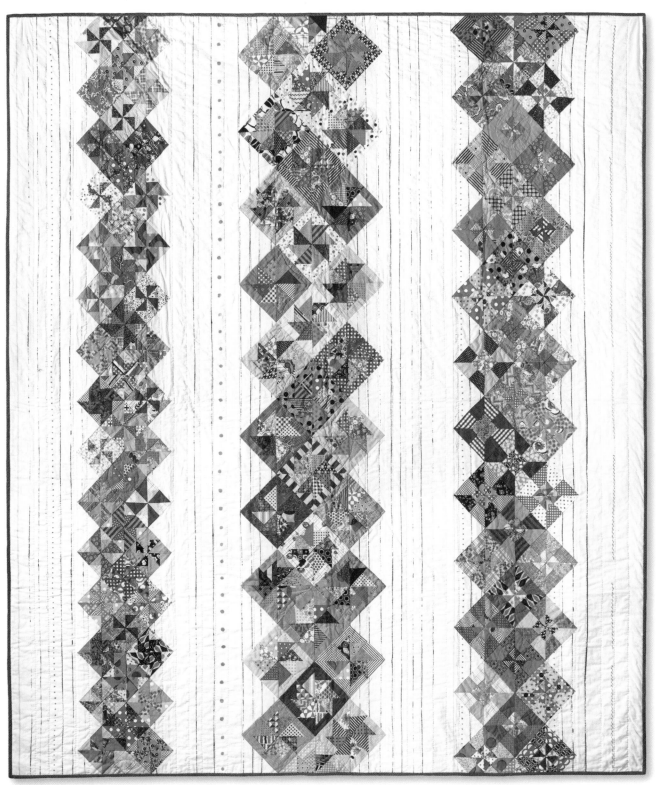

▲ **Spinning Around,** 75" × 84¾" (190.5cm × 213.4cm)
Quilted by Lucy Kingwell

For the Boys

❖ Quilt measures 67" (170.2cm) square

This is a great quilt for those big or small boys in your life. Its simple construction makes it a great project for beginners, and no special rulers or templates are required!

▼ MATERIALS & SUPPLIES

3 yds. (2.7m) total fabric or 31 fat eighths of a variety of fabrics for blocks

2 yds. (1.8m) dark fabric for sashing and binding

1¼ yds. (1.1m) light fabric for sashing

4¼ yds. (3.9m) fabric for backing

2¼ yds. (2.1m) square of batting

Sewing machine

¼" (6mm) sewing machine foot

Matching cotton thread for sewing

Aurifil 12-weight thread for hand quilting

Rotary cutter

Cutting mat

Ruler

General sewing notions (pins, scissors, tape measure etc.)

This quilt is machine pieced. Cutting instructions include a ¼" (6mm) seam allowance.

Cutting Instructions
Finished block size is 5" (12.7cm).

Make 121 blocks total.

From colored fabrics, cut:
121 rectangles at 3½" × 5½" (8.9cm × 14cm) (1 per block)

242 rectangles at 1½" × 3½" (3.8cm × 8.9cm) (2 per block)

145 squares at 1½" (3.8cm) (1 per block, plus 24 extra in addition to the 121)

From light sashing fabric, cut:
120 rectangles at 1½" × 5½" (3.8cm × 14cm)

220 squares at 1½" (3.8cm)

From dark sashing fabric, cut:
144 rectangles at 1½" × 5½" (3.8cm × 14cm)

246 squares at 1½" (3.8cm)

Block Assembly

1 | Take two 1½" × 3½" (3.8cm × 8.9cm) rectangles of colored fabric and stitch a 1½" (3.8cm) dark sashing square to each end (*Figure 1*). Press the seams toward the dark squares.

2 | Stitch these units to either side of the matching 3½" × 5½" (8.9cm × 14cm) rectangle (*Figure 2*).

3 | Make 66 blocks with dark sashing squares and 55 blocks with light sashing squares.

Quilt Assembly

Note: *A design wall or a space to lay out your blocks is very helpful at this point.*

4 | Lay out your blocks in 11 vertical rows containing 11 blocks (*Figure 3*).

5 | Sew dark sashing strips between blocks with dark corner squares, and sew light sashing strips between blocks with light corner squares (*Figure 3*).

6 | Begin and end each row with a sashing strip (*Figure 3*). Press the seam allowances toward the sashing.

7 | Make 6 rows with dark sashing strips and 5 rows with light sashing strips.

8 | Once the block rows are completed, make vertical sashing strips containing 6 dark and 5 light strips with colored post squares between them.

Note: *Notice in the assembly diagram that each 1½" (3.8cm) colored post uses the same fabric as the block to its upper right.*

FIGURE 3

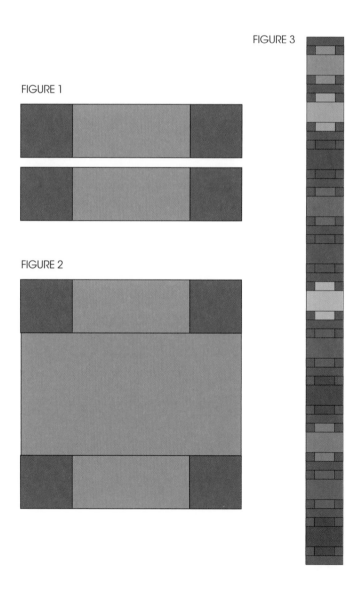

FIGURE 1

FIGURE 2

9 | Make 12 vertical sashing units. The post at the top of each unit will be one of the extra 24 colored squares you originally cut. The 12th sashing strip will be made up of the remaining extra squares. This will be the sashing strip on the right edge of the quilt.

10 | Stitch the rows together, alternating rows containing dark and light blocks. Press the seam allowances toward the sashing.

11 | Your quilt top is now complete. Baste before quilting.

Quilting

12 | Quilt as desired. I hand quilted this project with Aurifil 12-weight thread in diagonal rows going only one direction.

Binding

13 | Cut binding at 2½" (6.4cm) strips across the width of the fabric. Apply as a double binding.

Assembly Diagram

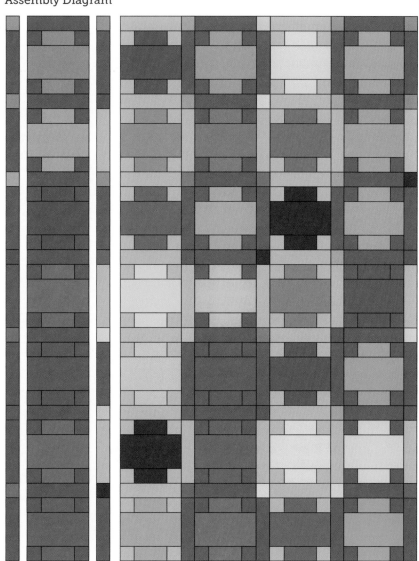

❖ Quilt measures 87" × 69" (220cm × 175cm)

Flea Market Dash

In this quilt, a traditional Churn Dash block is set on point and sashed. In some blocks, I chose to play with the color placement of lights, mediums and darks to create more interest. Traditionally, the background of the Churn Dash block was always lighter. By switching or partly switching the values, however, you can create blocks that look quite different and add to the charm of the quilt top. The fabric, Flea Market Fancy by Denyse Schmidt, gives the quilt a great vintage look. It is simple yet extremely effective.

▼ MATERIALS & SUPPLIES

6½ yds. (6m) total fabric of colored fabrics for blocks, posts and sashing

1½ yds. (1.4m) fabric for inset and corner triangles

¾ yd. (68.6cm) fabric for binding

5½ yds. (5m) fabric for backing

80" × 95" (2m × 2.4m) of batting

Sewing machine

¼" (6mm) sewing machine foot

Matching cotton thread for sewing

Perle 8-weight thread for hand quilting

Rotary cutter

Cutting mat

Ruler (18½" [47cm] square ruler recommended)

General sewing notions (pins, scissors, tape measure, etc.)

Cutting Instructions

Finished blocks will measure 10" (25.4cm) square.

Make 32 blocks total.

For each block, cut:

From light background fabric:
   2 squares at 4⅞" (12.4cm) (64 total)
   4 squares at 2½" (6.4cm) (128 total)

From darker fabric:
   2 squares at 4⅞" (12.4cm) (64 total)
   4 squares at 2½" (6.4cm) (128 total)

From center fabric:
   1 square at 2½" (6.4cm) (32 total)

From sashing fabric, cut:
   80 strips at 2½" × 10½" (6.4cm × 26.7cm)

For posts, cut from a variety of all fabrics:
   49 squares at 2½" (6.4cm)

For setting and corner triangles, cut:
   4 squares at 18¼" (46.4cm) (crosscut twice on the diagonal ⊠ to yield 14 setting triangles)

   2 squares at 10⅞" (27.6cm) (crosscut once on the diagonal ⊡ to yield 4 corner triangles)

Block Assembly

1 | Place 1 light 4⅞" (12.4cm) square and 1 dark 4⅞" (12.4cm) square with right sides together. Draw a diagonal line (solid line) and sew using a ¼" (6mm) seam on both sides of the diagonal line (dotted line) (*Figure 1*).

2 | Cut on the diagonal line and open to give 2 half-triangle squares (*Figure 2*). Repeat with the remaining 4⅞" (12.4cm) squares to make 4 half-triangle squares.

3 | Sew a dark 2½" (6.4cm) square to a light 2½" (6.4cm) square (*Figure 3*). Make 4.

4 | Sew the units together as shown in the block assembly diagram, adding the center square as you sew the middle row units.

   Make 32 blocks total.

Block Assembly Diagram

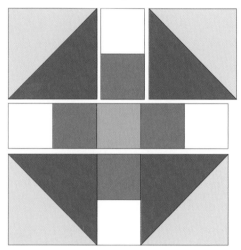

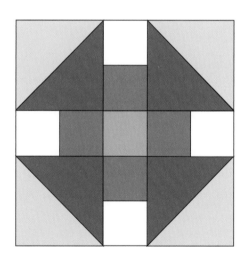

FIGURE 1

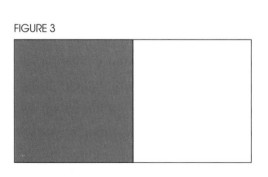

FIGURE 2

FIGURE 3

Layout Diagram

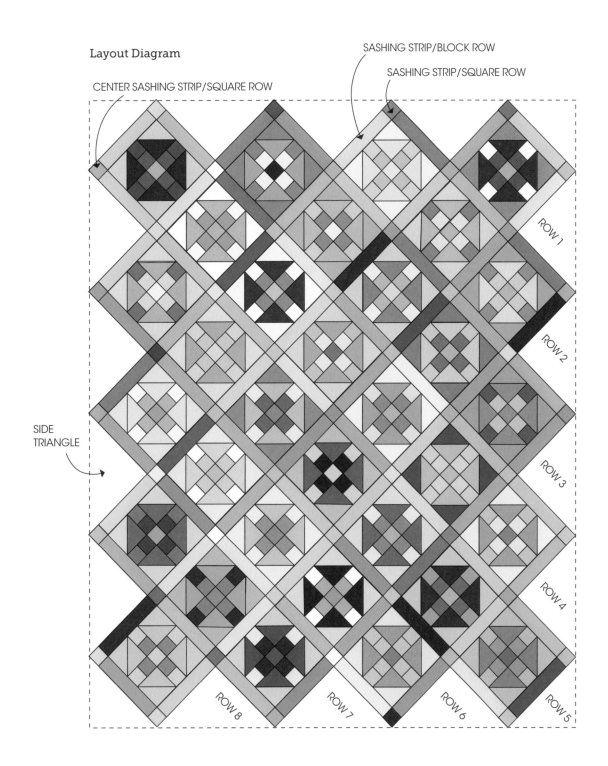

SASHING STRIP/BLOCK ROW

SASHING STRIP/SQUARE ROW

CENTER SASHING STRIP/SQUARE ROW

ROW 1

ROW 2

ROW 3

ROW 4

ROW 5

ROW 6

ROW 7

ROW 8

SIDE TRIANGLE

35

Quilt Assembly

5 | Following the layout diagram on page 35, lay out your blocks, sashing, posts, inset triangles and corner triangles in diagonal rows. As you lay out your quilt, work to achieve a pleasing color and value balance.

6 | Begin by joining the pieces, except for the setting and corner triangles, into diagonal rows. You are sewing two different kinds of rows. In one, blocks are joined to sashing strips, and in the other, the sashing strips are joined to posts, which creates long, skinny sashing rows. Press the seam allowances toward the sashing strips.

7 | Join the block rows to the long sashing-and-post rows. Use the row numbers in the layout diagram to determine on which side the sashing is joined to the rows. In rows 1–4, the sashing goes on the right side. In rows 5–8, the sashing goes on the left side. Do not join the center sashing strip to any of the rows yet.

8 | Add the setting triangles to the end of the rows.

Note: *The end of your triangle will extend past the edge of the block (Figure 4). This is necessary to ensure you have enough seam allowance.*

9 | Join the rows together to complete the quilt top. Sew rows 1–4 together, then add the center sashing-and-post row.

10 | Sew rows 5–8 together, then add that section to the other side of the center sashing-and-post row.

11 | Sew a corner triangle to each corner of your quilt top.

Your quilt top is now complete.

Quilting

12 | Quilt as desired. I used a combination of hand quilting and tying with Perle 8-weight thread in a variety of colors to complement the fabrics.

Binding

13 | Cut binding strips at 2½" (6.4cm) across the width of the fabric and apply it as a double binding.

FIGURE 4

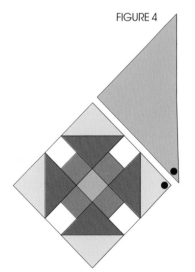

▲ **Flea Market Dash,** 87" × 69" (220cm × 175cm)

Spring Fever

❖ Quilt measures 60" × 72" (152cm × 183cm)

Over the past few years, I have been asked many times to design another quilt similar to my GREEN TEA AND SWEET BEANS pattern. I hope this is it!

I chose to hand piece and appliqué the blocks, and machine piece the checkerboard and quilt construction, but feel free to use the method of your choice.

▼ MATERIALS & SUPPLIES

2⅛ yds. (2m) fabric for scalloped edge and some backgrounds

½ yd. (46cm) total of 7 different fabrics for backgrounds

3–3½ yds. (2.7–3.2m) total of a large variety of color fabrics for appliqué and checkerboards: dots, stripes, florals, geometrics, etc. (fat sixteenths work well)

4" (10.2cm) fabric for butterfly bodies

4½ yds. (4.1m) fabric for backing

80" (2m) square of batting

Sewing machine

¼" (6mm) sewing machine foot

Matching cotton thread for sewing

Aurifil 12-weight thread for hand quilting

Rotary cutter

Cutting mat

Ruler (12½" [31.8cm] square recommended)

Freezer paper

Template plastic

⅜" (9mm) bias tape maker

General sewing notions (pins, scissors, tape measure, etc.)

Templates T7, T8, T9, T10, T11, T12, T13, T14, T15, T16, T17, T17 TOP, T17 BASE, T18, T18 TOP, T19, T19 TOP, T20, and T21 (on pattern sheet 2)

Cutting Instructions for Background and Borders
From the 2⅛ yd. (2m) length of fabric, cut:
4 strips at 2½" (6.4cm) by the length of fabric (for the scalloped borders)

From the background fabrics, cut:
23 squares at 13½" (34.3cm) (press registration marks onto these pieces as shown in Figure 1 to help you with the positioning of your appliqué)

4 rectangles 5½" × 13½" (14cm × 34.3cm)

FIGURE 1

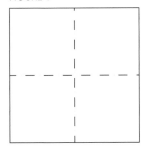

Appliqué Cutting Instructions for Flowers and Baskets

For appliqué pieces, cut:

27 from template T10 in various fabrics for buds and flower centers

15 from template T11 in various fabrics for buds and flower centers

16 from template T12 in various fabrics for flowers (fussy cut if desired)

5 from template T13 in various fabrics for flowers

15 from template T14 in various fabrics for flowers

9 from template T15 in various fabrics for flowers

42 from template T16 in various fabrics for leaves

2 different baskets from template T17, each with different bases and tops

3 different baskets from template T18, each with different tops

3 different baskets from template T19, each with different tops

2 different baskets from template T20

2 different baskets from template T21

FIGURE 2

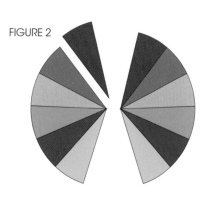

FIGURE 3

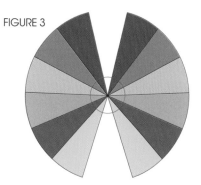

Butterfly Blocks

Make 12 blocks total.

For each butterfly, cut:

2 wedges from 6 different fabrics using template T7 (144 wedges total)

1 from template T8 for the butterfly body (12 bodies total)

1 | Stitch the wedges together, remembering to reverse the combination of fabrics so the wings are symmetrical (*Figure 2*).

2 | Center the wings on the background block using the registration lines. The points should overlap slightly as this will ensure the body will cover the raw tips (*Figure 3*).

3 | Trim the seam allowance to a scant ⅛" (3mm) at the point of the wings to remove bulk. Needle turn the appliqué in place.

4 | Position the body to cover the raw tips and appliqué in place.

5 | When complete, trim the blocks back to 12½" (31.8cm).

Basket Blocks

Make 11 blocks total (see appliqué cutting instructions).

6 | Using the circles T10, T11, T12, ovals T13, T14, T15, leaf T16 and baskets T17, T18, T19, T20, T21, create a design or use the appliqué layouts on pattern sheets 1 and 2 to create the appliqué designs on the project quilt.

7 | Make the stems from a variety of fabrics using the bias tape maker.

8 | You will need to appliqué the baskets in place first, leaving the top edge unstitched to slip the stems beneath the basket fabric.

9 | Appliqué the stems next, followed by the flowers (second) and the leaves (last). The flowers and the baskets will cover the ends of your stems.

10 | When complete, trim the blocks back to 12½" (31.8cm).

End Blocks
Make 4 blocks total.

11 | With the 5½" × 13½" (14cm × 34.3cm) rectangle, and using the assembly diagram on page 42 as a guide, make 2 posie blocks and 2 vine blocks.

12 | When complete, trim the blocks back to 5" × 12½" (12.7cm × 31.8cm).

Checkerboard blocks
Make 22 blocks total.

Checkerboard blocks are a great way to use your stash. Most of my stash consists of 12" (30.5cm) cuts, so I found it convenient to cut strips at 12" × 1½" (30.5cm × 3.8cm).

13 | Sew 3 strips together and, from these, cut strips at 1½" (3.8cm) (*Figure 4*).

14 | Make up strip sets in a variety of fabrics, then mix and match. Alternately, you can cut squares at 1½" (3.8cm) and stitch them together in threes.

15 | Make checkerboards of 12 squares across by 3 squares down (*Figure 5*). Make 22 checkerboard blocks total.

16 | Press the seams in alternate directions for each strip (for one strip, press seams outward; for the next strip, press them toward the center. Repeat). This will ensure your seam allowances come together nicely.

Quilt Assembly
17 | Join the blocks together in vertical rows. See the Assembly Diagram on page 42.

Backing
18 | Stitch the backing together. Before basting, cut 4 strips at 2½" (3.8cm) by the length of the fabric. There should be enough fabric for this. These strips will be used to back the scalloped edge.

19 | Baste and quilt as desired, but leave ½"–¾" (1.3cm–1.9cm) unquilted at each edge of the quilt. This is necessary to add the scalloped

FIGURE 4

FIGURE 5

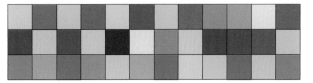

edges. (If you are having your quilt commercially machine quilted, you will use an alternate method of adding the scallops. See page 45.)

Quilting
20 | Quilt as desired. I hand quilted this project with Aurifil 12-weight thread in natural cream. I echo quilted the basket and butterflies and crossed the checkerboards.

Scalloped Edge Binding
21 | Take the previously cut strips of fabric and trim to the following:
  2 at 2½" × 72½" (6.4cm × 184.2cm)
  2 at 2½" × 60½" (6.4cm × 153.7cm)

22 | Cut strips of freezer paper at the following sizes:
  2 at 2" × 72½" (5.1cm × 184.2cm)
  2 at 2" × 60½" (5.1cm × 153.7cm)

Assembly Diagram

Note: *If your freezer paper is not long enough, join the pieces by overlapping about 1" (2.5cm) and pressing them together. It will peel off your ironing board easily.*

23 | Take these strips of freezer paper and draw a ¼" (6mm) line at each end (*Figure 6*).

24 | Measure down ⅞" (2.2cm) from the top of the paper and draw a line along the length (*Figure 6*).

25 | Mark the paper at 3" (7.6cm) intervals from the ¼" (6mm) line (*Figure 6*).

26 | Place circle template T9 over the marked paper strip until the edge of the circle intersects with the ⅞" (2.2cm) line. Draw a curved line (*Figure 7*). Trim the freezer paper, extending to the ¼" 6mm) seam allowance marked earlier (*Figure 8*).

27 | Align the bottom of the freezer paper with the lower edge of the scallop fabric strips. Press the freezer paper to the wrong side of the strips. You will have extra fabric at the top.

28 | Place the backing fabric strip right sides together with the scallop strip, then place a 2½" (6.4cm) strip of batting behind the wrong side of the backing strip.

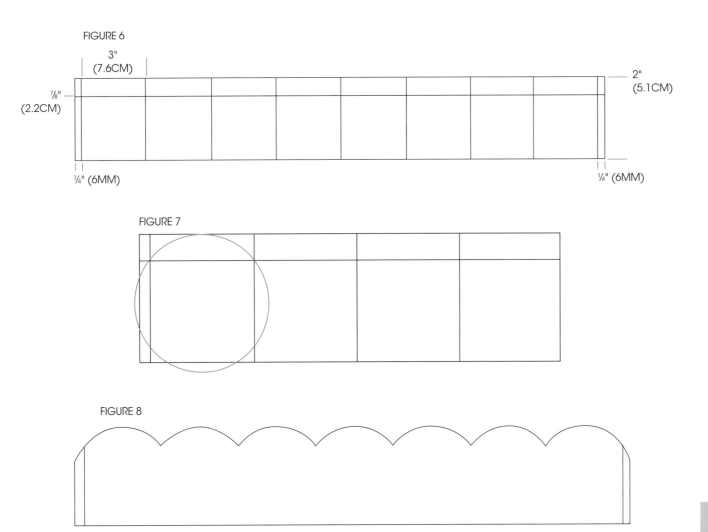

FIGURE 6

FIGURE 7

FIGURE 8

29 | Stitch around the edge of the freezer paper template. You will get a better result if you make 1 straight stitch at the base of the scallops (*Figure 9*).

30 | Trim, leaving a scant ¼" (6mm) seam allowance around the scalloped edge. Trim the batting back within the seam allowance.

31 | Clip the seam allowance into the base of the scallop. Be careful not to clip the stitches (*Figure 10*).

32 | Turn right-side out and press. Make 4 scalloped edges total.

33 | Using your ruler and rotary cutter, align the ruler with the ⅜" (1cm) on the inner curve of the scallops. Trim your strips. This will allow your scallops to sit just above the edge of the quilt when stitched and turned out (*Figure 11*).

Attaching Scallops
34 | Trim the backing and batting even with the edge of the quilt.

FIGURE 9

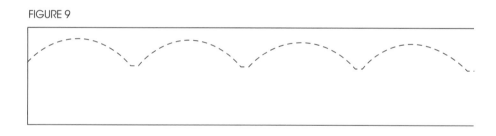

FIGURE 10

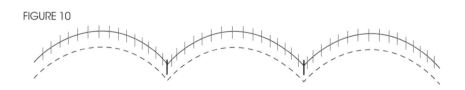

35 | Before you stitch the scalloped edges in place, fold your backing fabric out of the way and tack.

36 | Stitch the scallops in place with right sides together, aligning the raw edges. The corners should sit flat beside each other (*Figure 12*).

37 | Turn and press.

38 | Remove the basting stitches from the backing. Fold the seam allowance under and slip stitch or appliqué it in place, covering the seam allowance of the scallop.

39 | Complete the quilting to the edges.

For Commercial Machine Quilting

If you decide to have your quilt commercially machine quilted, the quilting will extend to the edges and you won't be able to fold your backing out of the way. For this, use the following method:

1 | Cut 4 strips of backing fabric at 1½" × 73" (3.8cm × 185.4cm) (or to the length of your backing).

FIGURE 11

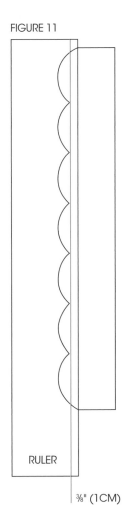

RULER

⅜" (1CM)

FIGURE 12

2 | Press the fabric in half, folded down the length with the right sides out.

3 | Prepare the quilt and scalloped edge as before in steps 23–34. Place the scalloped borders and quilt with the right sides together. Place the backing strips on top (they will be sitting on the wrong side of the scallop). All raw edges should align (*Figure 13*).

4 | Stitch with ¼" (6mm) seam allowance. Stitch the top and bottom scallops on first, turn and press. The fold of the backing strip will now sit down over the seam allowance. Slipstitch in place.

5 | Repeat the process with the side borders. Remember to fold a small seam allowance at each end of the folded strip. Fold this to the front before stitching. When you flip this over, the seam allowance will be underneath the strip and will create a neat corner (*Figure 14*).

Your quilt top is now complete.

FIGURE 13

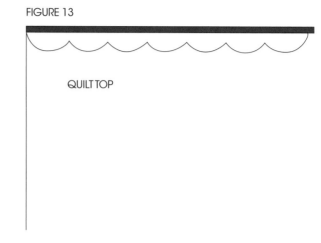

QUILT TOP

FIGURE 14

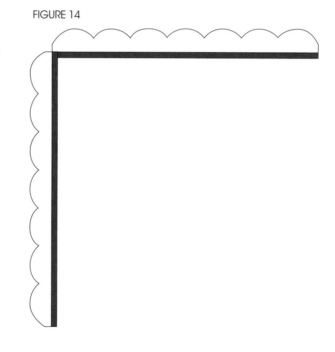

▲ **Spring Fever,** 60" × 72" (152cm × 183cm)

❖ Finished quilt measures 59" × 67" (150cm × 170cm)

Bonnie Lass

This little beauty is simple to make but incredibly appealing. Setting these simple blocks on point adds a lot of movement and interest. This quilt is easy to resize simply by changing the number of blocks you make.

▼ MATERIALS & SUPPLIES

2 yds. (1.8m) total fabric of a large variety of feature fabrics (prints, solids, dots, stripes, etc.)

2 yds. (1.8m) total of background fabrics (remember to look at the reverse side as sometimes this is a good option)

⅝ yd. (0.6m) fabric for setting triangles

⅝ yd. (0.6m) fabric for binding

4 yds. (3.7m) fabric for backing

71" × 75" (1.8m × 1.9m) batting

Sewing machine

¼" (6mm) sewing machine foot

Matching cotton thread for sewing

Machine quilting thread or hand sewing thread, as preferred

Rotary cutter

Cutting mat

Ruler

General sewing notions (pins, scissors, tape measure, etc.)

This quilt is machine pieced. Cutting instructions include a ¼" (6mm) seam allowance.

Cutting Instructions
Make 98 blocks total.

Finished block measures 6" (15.2cm)

For each block, cut:
4 rectangles at 2" × 3½" (5.1cm × 8.9cm) from background fabric (392 total)

4 rectangles at 2" × 3½" (5.1cm × 8.9cm) from feature fabrics (392 total)

You will need a total of 784 rectangles of both background fabric and feature fabrics.

BLOCK ASSEMBLY
1 | Pair 1 background rectangle and 1 feature rectangle (*Figure 1*). Make 4.

2 | Stitch these 4 units together, alternating the vertical and horizontal orientation (*Figure 2*). Make 98 blocks total.

FIGURE 1

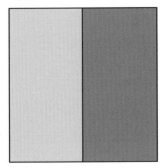

FIGURE 2

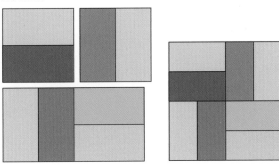

Quilt Assembly

3 | Lay out the blocks to get an even distribution of color and print. Remember, you are setting these blocks on point (*Figure 3*). Layout should be 7 blocks across the top by 8 blocks down the side (to make the size shown).

FIGURE 3

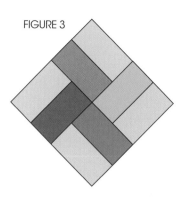

Assembly Diagram (Rows)

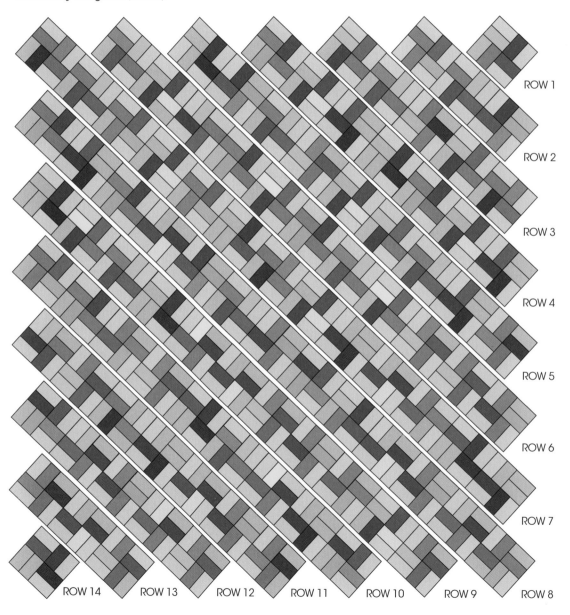

ROW 1

ROW 2

ROW 3

ROW 4

ROW 5

ROW 6

ROW 7

ROW 14   ROW 13   ROW 12   ROW 11   ROW 10   ROW 9   ROW 8

Row 1: 1 Block	Row 8: 13 Blocks
Row 2: 3 Blocks	Row 9: 11 Blocks
Row 3: 5 Blocks	Row 10: 9 Blocks
Row 4: 7 Blocks	Row 11: 7 Blocks
Row 5: 9 Blocks	Row 12: 5 Blocks
Row 6: 11 Blocks	Row 13: 3 Blocks
Row 7: 13 Blocks	Row 14: 1 Block

Stitch the blocks together in rows according to the row and block numbers above (compare to the assembly diagram for a visual aid), then add setting triangles as described below.

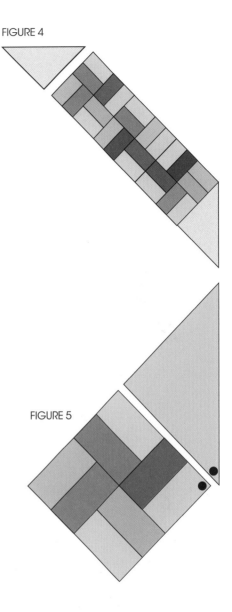

FIGURE 4

FIGURE 5

Setting Triangles
From your chosen fabric, cut:

7 squares at 9¾" (24.8cm) cut twice on the diagonal ⊠

2 squares at 5⅛" (13cm) cut once on the diagonal ◫ (these are for the 4 corners)

4 | Add the 9¾" (24.8cm) triangles to the end of each row (*Figure 4*).

Note: *The end of your triangle will extend past the edge of the block* (Figure 5). *This is necessary to ensure you have enough seam allowance.*

5 | Stitch the rows together and add your corner triangles last (see the diagram on page 52).

Your quilt top is now complete.

Quilting
6 | Baste and quilt as desired. I had this project professionally machine quilted.

Binding
7 | Cut the binding fabric into strips that measure 2½" (6.4cm) by the width of fabric. Apply as a double binding.

Assembly Diagram (Finishing)

▲ **Bonnie Lass,** 59" × 67" (150cm × 170cm)
Quilted by Kylie Cannon of Finely Finished Quilts

Daisy Do

I love this quilt, which is made from a repeat daisy block. It's a great quilt to showcase a variety of your favorite fabrics.

▼ MATERIALS & SUPPLIES

Approx. 4 yds. (3.7m) total of a large variety of print, pattern and solid fabrics (fat eighths and fat sixteenths work well)

2¼ yds. (2.1m) fabric for background

4 yds. (3.7m) fabric for backing

⅝ yd. (0.6m) fabric for binding

70" × 76" (177.8cm × 193cm) batting

Template plastic

Matching cotton thread for sewing

Aurifil 12-weight thread

Rotary cutter

Cutting mat

Ruler

General sewing notions (pins, scissors, tape measure, etc.)

Templates T29, T30, T31, T32, T33, T33 REVERSE, T34, T34 REVERSE and T35 (on pattern sheet 1)

This quilt is hand pieced. Draw your stitching line around the templates, then add your seam allowance.

Cutting Instructions

Note: *Remember to note the grainline.*

Makes 77 full daisies and 8 half daisies.

For each daisy, cut:

6 of template T29 from one fabric (494 total)

6 of template T30 from a different fabric (486 total)

1 of template T31 from a third fabric (77 total)

From the background fabric, cut:

4 borders at 4½" (11.4cm) wide by the length of the fabric (set these pieces aside)

From the remainder of background fabric, cut:

220 from connector template T32

16 from edge template T33

16 from template T33 REVERSE

2 from corner template T34

2 from template T34 REVERSE

10 from edge template T35

Block Assembly

1 | Stitch a T30 piece to the right-hand side of a T29 piece. Remember to note the registration marks (*Figure 1*). Make 6 units.

2 | Stitch these 6 units into a circle to create a daisy (*Figure 2*).

Note: *When stitching, start at the center points. This is one time you don't need to fuss about getting the center junction perfect because it will be covered with the appliquéed circle. Press the seam allowances toward the T30 pieces.*

3 | Make 77 daisy blocks and 8 half daisy blocks (shown in *Figure 3*).

4 | For the half daisy, press the seam allowances toward the T29 pieces on the lower edge to retain the seam allowance. The lower edge will be trimmed back. Remember to retain your ¼" (6mm) seam allowance.

5 | Appliqué a T31 piece onto the center of the full daisy blocks (*Figure 4*).

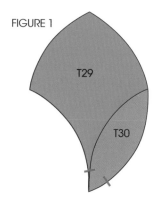

FIGURE 1

T29

T30

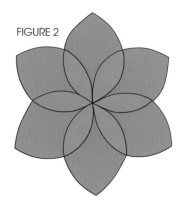

FIGURE 2

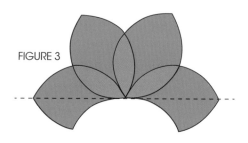

FIGURE 3

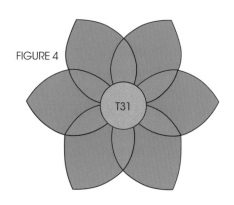

FIGURE 4

T31

Assembly Diagram

Quilt Assembly

6 | Lay out your daisies to get an even distribution of color, value and pattern. A design wall is a very useful tool at this stage.

You will have 5 rows containing 9 daisies and 4 rows with 8 full daises and a half daisy at each end (see the diagram on page 57).

7 | Stitch the rows together with a connector T32 piece (*Figure 5*).

8 | At the end of each row that has 9 daisies, stitch a T35 piece (*Figure 6*).

9 | Once you have completed stitching the rows, stitch connector T32 pieces to the right side of rows 1–8, but not the 9th row.

10 | Stitch the rows together to form the body of the quilt.

11 | Make 2 edge rows as described in the following instructions (*Figure 7*).

For each edge row, cut:

8 of template T29, trimmed at the dotted line (remember to add a ¼" [6mm] seam allowance).

You will also use the previously cut T33 and T34 pieces for the following instructions.

12 | Lay these out beside the body of the quilt to make sure you stitch them correctly.

13 | You should have 2 completely straight edges. Stitch in place.

14 | Trim your previously cut borders as described below. (Check the quilt's measurements first, as discussed in Borders in Appendix B).

2 at 4½" × 60½" (11.4cm × 153.7cm). Stitch these pieces to each side of your quilt.

2 at 4½" × 62½" (11.4cm × 158.8cm). Stitch these pieces to the top and bottom of your quilt.

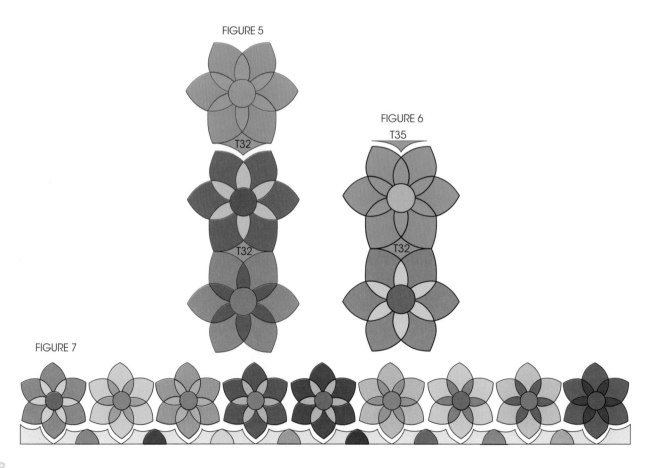

FIGURE 5

FIGURE 6

FIGURE 7

Assembly Diagram (with edge rows)

Quilting

15 | Your quilt top is now complete. Baste and quilt as desired. I hand quilted this project with Aurifil 12-weight thread as shown in Figure 8 and Figure 9.

Binding

16 | Cut the binding into 2½" (6.4cm) strips across the width of the fabric. Apply as a double binding.

FIGURE 9

FIGURE 8

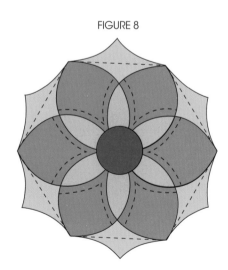

▲ **Daisy Do,** 68" × 62" (173cm × 157cm)

Flutterby

Being the mother of daughters, I see this as a butterfly quilt, but my friends who have sons see spacecraft. This quilt is easy, cute and gender-neutral!

▼ MATERIALS & SUPPLIES

2 yds. (1.9m) total of a variety of colored fabrics, including checks, spots, stripes, florals, etc.

2⅞ yds. (2.6m) of white fabric

½ yd. (0.5m) of black and white check-ered fabric

1¼ yds. (1m) fabric total in of a variety of beige and taupe fabrics

½ yd. (.5m) fabric for binding

4 yds. (3.7m) fabric for backing

70" (1.8m) square of batting

Sewing machine

¼" (6mm) sewing machine foot

Matching cotton thread for sewing

Perle 8-weight thread for hand quilting

Template plastic

Marker

Rotary cutter

Cutting mat

Ruler

General sewing notions (pins, scissors, tape measure, etc.)

Template T46 (on pattern sheet 1)

A ¼" (6mm) seam allowance is included in all cutting instructions.

Cutting Instructions
Finished block measures 10½" (26.7cm)

From the colored fabrics, cut:
132 rectangles at 5½" × 3" (14cm × 7.6cm)
104 squares at 2¼" (5.7cm)

From the beige fabrics, cut:
300 squares at 2¼" (5.7cm)

From the checkered fabric, cut:
100 squares at 2¼" (5.7cm)

From the white fabric, cut:
8 strips 2¼" (5.7cm) wide by the length of the fabric. Put these strips aside for borders.

132 rectangles at 5½" × 3" (14cm × 7.6cm)

Block Assembly

1 | Place the colored rectangles together in pairs, right sides together. Crosscut once on the diagonal. This will ensure half of the triangles are reversed.

Repeat the process with the white rectangles.

2 | Stitch a colored and a white triangle together to create a rectangle (*Figure 1*). Make 66 rectangles and 66 rectangles in the reverse color arrangement (132 in total). Press the seams toward the colored fabric.

3 | Make template T46 in template plastic (must be transparent). The template must measure 4" × 2¼" (10.2cm × 5.7cm). Mark each corner at the ¼" (6mm) junction (*Figure 2*).

4 | With right sides facing, place your rectangles and your template together with diagonally opposing dots on the seamline (*Figure 3*).

5 | Draw around the template. Trim on the line and discard the excess. Repeat on all rectangles (this creates a perfect ¼" [6mm] seam allowance).

FIGURE 1

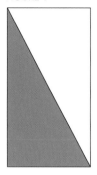

FIGURE 2

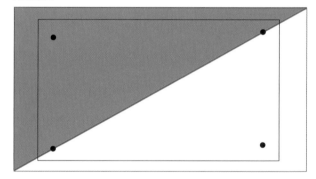

FIGURE 3

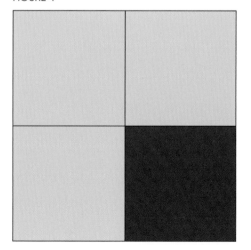

FIGURE 4

FIGURE 5

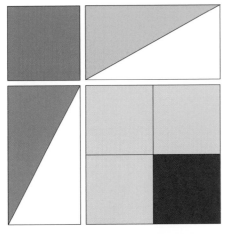

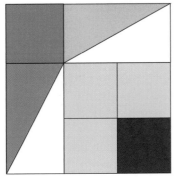

FIGURE 6

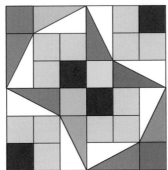

6 | Make a four-patch block with 3 beige squares and 1 checkered square (*Figure 4*). Make 100 blocks.

7 | Lay out your unit pieces to get a pleasing mix of colors and patterns. Stitch them together as shown in Figure 5.

8 | Make 4 of these units per finished Flutterby block using a mix of your colored fabrics.

9 | Stitch the units together as shown in Figure 6. Make 25 Flutterby blocks.

Quilt Assembly

10 | Lay out the blocks to give a pleasing mix of colors and patterns. Stitch together in 5 rows of 5 blocks.

Borders

BORDER 1
From the previously cut white strips, cut:
  2 borders at 2¼" × 53" (5.7cm × 134.6cm)
  2 borders at 2¼" × 56½" (5.7cm × 143.5cm)

11 | Stitch the shorter borders to each side of the quilt. Stitch the longer borders to the top and bottom of the quilt. Press the seams to the outer edge of the quilt top.

BORDER 2
12 | Stitch the remainder of your half-triangle rectangles as shown in Figure 7 to make 4 borders, each with 16 half-triangle rectangles. Finished borders should measure 56½" (143.5cm), including seam allowance.

13 | Stitch 2 of these borders to each side of your quilt.

14 | Take the 4 colored squares previously cut and stitch them to each end of the remaining borders. Stitch these borders to the top and bottom of your quilt top.

15 | Press the seam allowances toward the white border.

BORDER 3
From previously cut white strips, cut:
  2 borders at 60" (152.4cm)
  2 borders at 63½" (161.3cm)

16 | Stitch the shorter borders to each side of the quilt. Stitch the longer borders to the top and bottom of the quilt. Press the seams to the outer edge of the quilt top.

Quilting
17 | I quilted this project with Perle 8-weight thread in a variety of colors to complement the "butterflies" (as shown in Figure 8).

Binding
18 | Cut the binding into 2½" (6.4cm) strips across the width of the fabric. Apply as a double binding.

FIGURE 7

FIGURE 8

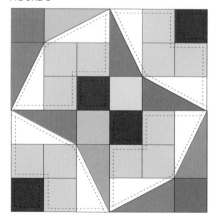

▲ **Flutterby,** 63" (160cm) square

chapter 2

Pillows

These pillow patterns are great for beginners who may find starting a larger project daunting. Sometimes a smaller, quicker project to complete will spur you on and hold your interest! These smaller projects are also spectacular gifts to a special friend or loved one. A quick and easy way to update any space, a few throw pillows will add a spark to your sofa. I like an eclectic mix of patterns. Try a combination of some pieced and some made from a single fabric with a great print design. Different-sized square and rectangular pillows will add great dimension and create a very personal touch.

In this next section are six pillow designs, all made with a repeat block so you can make any size you wish. You can even use the blocks to make a king-size quilt or choose just part of the design to create an adorable crib quilt.

I have included a simple method of making a pillow with an interesting back detail to hide the zipper.

Wheel of Fortune

❖ Finished pillow measures 22½" (57.2cm) square

I absolutely love this pillow, and after making four blocks, I wanted desperately to keep going and make a quilt. Alas, I didn't have enough background fabric.

These little wheels are foundation pieced and quite easy once you get going. Just make sure when choosing your background fabric that it's a stable fabric and doesn't have too much stretch. My first block used linen as the background, and once the foundation was removed, it didn't hold its shape very well and had to be discarded.

▼ MATERIALS & SUPPLIES

⅞ yd. (80cm) background fabric

½ yd. (46cm) total of colored fabrics (small cuts and some strips to cut the 11¼" [28.6cm] long sashing)

⅔ yd. (61cm) fabric for backing

22" (55.9cm) zipper

Sewing machine

¼" (6mm) sewing machine foot

Zipper foot

Matching cotton thread for sewing

Quilting thread (optional)

Foundation paper of choice

Rotary cutter

Cutting mat

Ruler

General sewing notions (pins, scissors, tape measure, etc.)

Seam ripper (handy for removing stubborn papers)

Template plastic

Templates T44, T45 (on pattern sheet 1)

A ¼" (6mm) seam allowance is included in all rotary cutting instructions. For template instructions, please add a seam allowance after tracing the design.

Cutting Instructions for Blocks
Finished block measures 10¾" (27.3cm)

From background fabric, cut:
1½"-wide (3.8cm) strips, then cut these strips into 4" (10.2cm) lengths (96 rectangles total)

16 of template T44

16 of template T45

5 squares at 1¼" (3.2cm)

From colored fabric cut:
Cut 80 strips at 1½" × 4" (3.8cm × 10.2cm)

Cut 16 strips at 1¼" × 5½" (3.2cm × 14cm)

Cut 4 strips at 1¼" × 11¼" (3.2cm × 28.6cm)

Block Assembly
Refer to the foundation piecing notes in Appendix A, if needed.

1 | Trace your foundation template onto your paper foundation. You will need to trace 16 pieces, or trace 1 and photocopy the others. You only need to trace the center wedge template (the section between T44 and T45 on the template).

Note: *Your wedges begin and end with background fabric. Alternate colored and background rectangles.*

2 | Align a background strip and your foundation piece with right sides facing out (the wrong side of the fabric should be against the unprinted side of the paper).

3 | Place a colored strip on top of the background strip with the right sides together.
   Note: *This is where most people make a mistake, and it's easy to have the fabrics positioned incorrectly. When you flip your colored strip, it must cover the foundation. You will find it easier if you lay your foundation on a flat surface, fold it back on the line you are going to stitch and check to be sure you have a ¼" (6mm) seam allowance extending past this line.*

4 | Stitch on the printed line, extending slightly past the paper (*Figure 1*). Be sure to backstitch, as it will prevent your stitches from unravelling when you remove the foundation papers.

5 | Trim this seam allowance to ¼" (6mm). Don't worry about excess fabric at the top and bottom. Do not trim through the paper.

6 | Flip the colored fabric and press. Fold the foundation paper back on the next seam line and trim the colored fabric, leaving a ¼" (6mm) seam allowance beyond the folded paper. Take a background strip and align the edges with right sides together. Stitch, flip, press and repeat steps 4–6 until the wedge is completed (*Figure 2*).
   Make 16 total.

7 | Trim the excess fabric that extends past the paper, leaving a ¼" (6mm) seam allowance beyond the foundation paper on all sides (*Figure 3*).

8 | Pin and mark the centers of the T44 and T45 pieces (*Figure 4*).

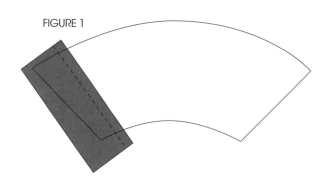

FIGURE 1

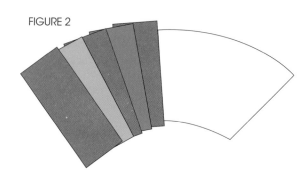

FIGURE 2

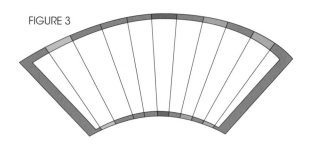

FIGURE 3

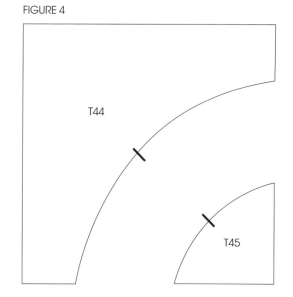

FIGURE 4

T44

T45

9 | Pin the pieces together, matching the center of your pieced wedge.

10 | Stitch the pieces in place, sewing along the edge of the paper but not on the paper (*Figure 5*).
  Make 16 units total.

11 | Gently remove the foundation papers, being careful not to disrupt the stitches.

12 | Take 2 units and stitch with a 1¼" × 5½" (3.2cm × 14cm) colored sashing strip between them (*Figure 6*).
  Repeat to make 8 of these units.

13 | Stitch two 5½" (14cm) strips together with a 1¼" (3.2cm) square of background fabric between them (*Figure 7*).
  Make 4 of these units.

14 | Stitch the units together as shown in Figure 8.
  Make 4 blocks.

FIGURE 5

FIGURE 6

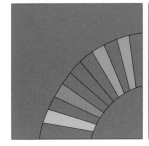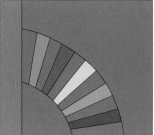

FIGURE 7

FIGURE 8

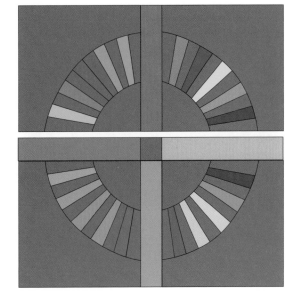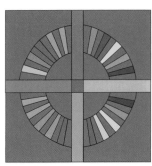

15 | Repeat this process with the blocks and the 11¼" (28.6cm) long strips (*Figure 9*).

16 | Your pillow top is now complete. Follow the pilllow assembly instructions at the end of this chapter or, if you wish to make a quilt using this design, keep repeating the process until you have the size you desire.

Quilting

17 | Quilt if desired before assembling the cushion (I chose not to quilt this pillow).

One quilting option would be to quilt in concentric circles, as shown in Figure 11, then stitch in the ditch along the wedges.

-----------------MAKE IT A QUILT

One option for making this into a quilt would be to stitch your blocks together in rows with sashing in between. Then make long horizontal sashing to place between each row of blocks (*Figure 10*).

Each block uses approximately 8" (20.3cm) of background fabric and one fat eighth of colored fabric in total. Use these measurements as a guide for your fabric requirements when planning larger projects.

FIGURE 9

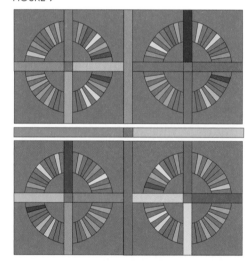

FIGURE 10

FIGURE 11

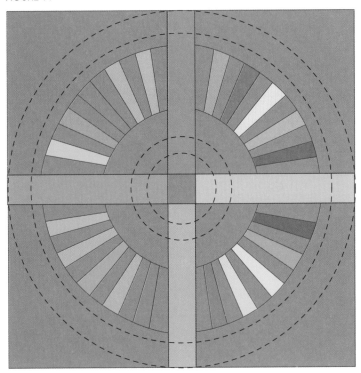

▲ **Wheel of Fortune,** 22½" square (57.2cm)

◆ Finished pillow measures 23" × 30" (58.4 × 76.2cm)

She Loves You

This design is a twist on the classic Courthouse Step block. You can make this pillow as I did, or you can make more blocks to create a quilt of any size. A crib quilt for a baby girl would be adorable!

▼ MATERIALS & SUPPLIES

⅝ yd. (57cm) total of colored fabrics in a wide variety of colors and patterns

¾ yd. (68cm) total of neutrals/low-volume fabrics in a wide variety of tones and patterns

¾ yd. (68cm) fabric for backing

22" (56cm) zipper

Sewing machine

¼" (6mm) sewing machine foot

Zipper foot

Matching cotton thread

Rotary cutter

Cutting mat

Ruler

General sewing notions (pins, scissors, tape measure, etc.)

A ¼"(6mm) seam allowance is included in all cutting instructions.

Note: *Each heart is made of 3 different Courthouse Step blocks measuring 3½" (8.9cm) each. For each heart, make 2 of Block A, 1 of Block B and 1 of Block C. The finished block measures 7" (17.8cm).*

Block A Cutting Instructions

Make 2 of block A per Heart block (see Figure 4 on page 79).

From the neutral fabrics, cut:

2 squares at 1" (2.5cm) (4 total)

3 rectangles at 1" × 2" (2.5cm × 5.1cm) (6 total)

3 rectangles at 1" × 3" (2.5cm × 7.6cm) (6 total)

1 rectangle at 1" × 4" (2.5cm × 10.2cm) (2 total)

From the colored fabrics, cut:

1 square at 1" (2.5cm) (2 total)

1 rectangle at 1" × 2" (2.5cm × 5.1cm) (2 total)

1 rectangle at 1" × 3" (2.5cm × 7.6cm) (2 total)

1 rectangle at 1" × 4" (2.5cm × 10.2cm) (2 total)

FIGURE 1

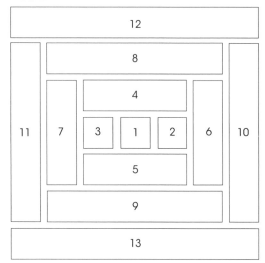

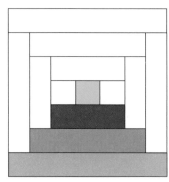

BLOCK A ASSEMBLY

1 | Sew together in the order shown in Figure 1.

Block B Cutting Instructions

Make 1 of block B per Heart block (see Figure 4 on page 79).

From the neutral fabrics, cut:

1 square at 1" (2.5cm)

1 rectangle at 1" × 1½" (2.5cm × 3.8cm)

1 rectangle at 1" × 2" (2.5cm × 5.1cm)

1 rectangle at 1" × 2½" (2.5cm × 6.4cm)

1 rectangle at 1" × 3" (2.5cm × 7.6cm)

1 rectangle at 1" × 3½" (2.5cm × 8.9cm)

From the colored fabrics, cut:

1 square at 1" (2.5cm)

1 rectangle at 1" × 1½" (2.5cm × 3.8cm)

1 rectangle at 1" × 2" (2.5cm × 5.1cm)

1 rectangle at 1" × 2½" (2.5cm × 6.4cm)

1 rectangle at 1" × 3" (2.5cm × 7.6cm)

1 rectangle at 1" × 3½" (2.5cm × 8.9cm)

1 rectangle at 1" × 4" (2.5cm × 10.2cm)

BLOCK B ASSEMBLY

2 | Sew together in the order shown in Figure 2.

Block C

Make 1 of block C per Heart block (see Figure 4 on page 79).

From the neutral fabrics, cut:

1 square at 1" (2.5cm)

1 rectangle at 1" × 1½" (2.5cm × 3.8cm)

1 rectangle at 1" × 2" (2.5cm × 5.1cm)

1 rectangle at 1" × 2½" (2.5cm × 6.4cm)

1 rectangle at 1" × 3" (2.5cm × 7.6cm)

1 rectangle at 1" × 3½" (2.5cm × 8.9cm)

FIGURE 2

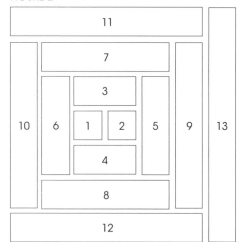

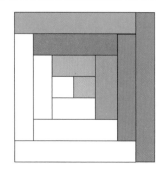

From the colored fabrics, cut:

1 square at 1" (2.5cm)

1 rectangle at 1" × 1½" (2.5cm × 3.8cm)

1 rectangle at 1" × 2" (2.5cm × 5.1cm)

1 rectangle at 1" × 2½" (2.5cm × 6.4cm)

1 rectangle at 1" × 3" (2.5cm × 7.6cm)

1 rectangle at 1" × 3½" (2.5cm × 8.9cm)

1 rectangle at 1" × 4" (2.5cm × 10.2cm)

BLOCK C ASSEMBLY

3 | Sew together in the order shown in Figure 3.

Heart Block Assembly

4 | Assemble the Heart block as shown in Figure 4. Make 12 blocks.

5 | Stitch the blocks together in 3 rows of 4 blocks, as shown in the assembly diagram on page 80.

6 | Cut 2 strips of neutral fabric 1½" × 21½" (3.8cm × 54.6cm) and stitch to each side. Press the seams toward the strip.

7 | Cut 2 strips of neutral fabric 1½" × 30½" (3.8cm × 77.5cm) and stitch to the top and bottom. Press the seams toward the strip.

8 | Your pillow top is now complete. Follow the instructions at the end of the chapter to complete the assembly of your pillow.

If you choose to make a quilt, add the desired number of blocks before adding sashing strips or borders.

FIGURE 3

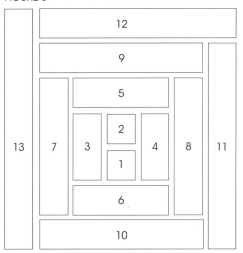

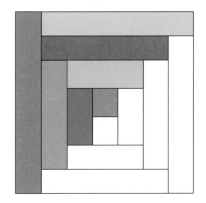

FIGURE 4

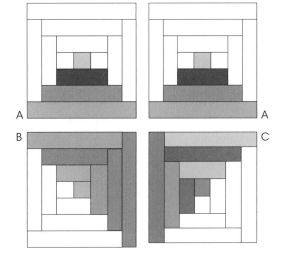

Assembly Diagram

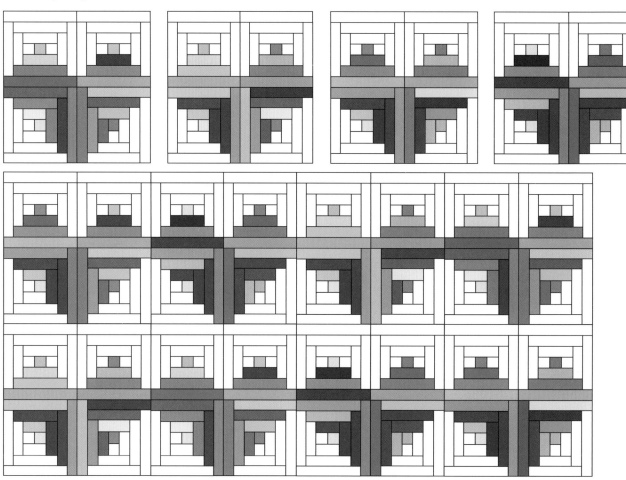

▲ **She Loves You,** 23" × 30" (58.4cm × 76.2cm)

-----------**MAKE SINGLE BLOCKS**
Make a colorful and practical gift by creating single Heart blocks and turning them into pot holders!

Home Run

This pillow is made from the age-old Kansas Dugout block pattern. It demonstrates that color doesn't need to be bright to be effective by using a low-volume color palette.

I chose to hand piece this design and keep the squares as whole pieces, but if you wish to machine piece it's very easy to construct. I've included instructions for both methods.

▼ MATERIALS & SUPPLIES

½ yd. (46cm) total of light fabrics

¼ yd. (23cm) total of darker fabrics for contrast squares and triangles

⅝ yd. (57cm) fabric for backing

18" (46cm) zipper

Template plastic

Sewing machine

¼" (6mm) sewing machine foot

Zipper foot

Rotary cutter

Cutting mat

Ruler

Matching cotton thread for sewing

Quilting thread (optional)

General sewing notions (pins, scissors, tape measure, etc.)

Templates T26, T27 and T28 (on pattern sheet 1)

Instructions for hand piecing require you to add a ¼" (6mm) seam allowance. The machine-pieced instructions already include this allowance.

Cutting Instructions for Hand Piecing

From the lighter fabrics, cut:

36 pieces from a variety of fabrics using template T26

From the darker fabrics, cut:

13 pieces from a variety of fabrics using template T27

8 pieces from template T28

4 pieces from half of template T28 (*Figure 1*) (don't forget to add a ¼" (6mm) seam allowance around the half template)

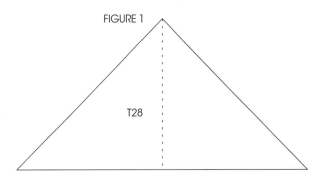
FIGURE 1

T28

Hand-piecing Assembly

1 | Stitch a T26 piece to either side of a T27 piece (*Figure 2*).

2 | Add the remaining pieces to opposite sides, completing the mitered seams (*Figure 3*). Make 9 units.

3 | Stitch the blocks together, making 3 rows of 3 blocks (*Figure 4*).

4 | Stitch the rows together, inserting T27 pieces between rows and T28 pieces at the edges.

Complete by adding the smaller triangles cut from the T28 half template to the corners (*Figure 5*).

5 | After you've completed 9 blocks, stitch them together in 3 rows containing 3 blocks as shown in the assembly diagram.

6 | Your pillow top is now complete. Quilt if desired.

7 | Complete your pillow using the instructions at the end of the chapter.

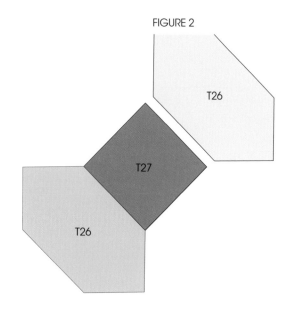

FIGURE 2

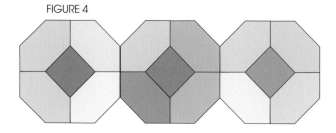

FIGURE 4

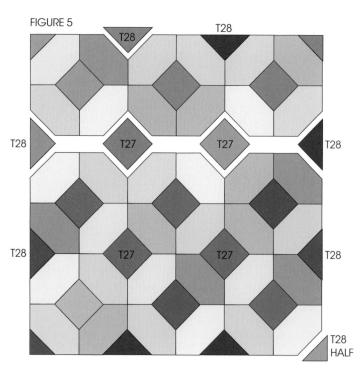

FIGURE 5

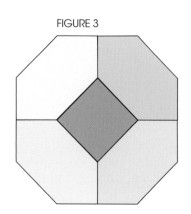

FIGURE 3

Cutting Instructions for Machine Piecing

A ¼" (6mm) seam allowance is included in the instructions below.

From the lighter fabrics cut:
36 squares at 4" (10.2cm)

From the darker fabrics, cut:
72 squares at 1¼" × 1¾" (3.2cm × 4.4cm).

Note: *You will need to cut 4 of each fabric because these will come together to create the squares between the hexagons.*

Machine Assembly

This method takes a little planning because the corner triangles need to come together to create the squares.

1 | Mark a diagonal line down the center on the wrong side of the 1¾" (4.4cm) squares.

2 | Take a 4" (10.2cm) square and place 2 of the 1¾" (4.4cm) squares right sides together in diagonally opposite corners. Stitch on the marked line and trim off the corners, leaving a ¼" (6mm) seam allowance. **Note:** *These 1¾" (4.4cm) squares will be different* (Figure 6).

3 | Press the triangles open to complete the corners.
   Repeat steps 5–7 with the remaining squares, remembering to follow your chosen sequence.

4 | Stitch the squares together to create a 7" (17.8cm) finished block (block will measure 7½" [19.1cm] with the seam allowance) (*Figure 7*).

FIGURE 6

FIGURE 7

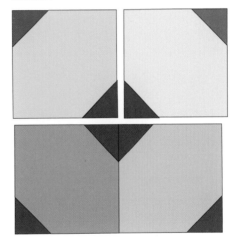

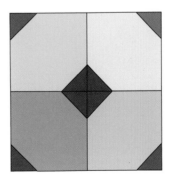

5 | After you've completed 9 blocks, stitch them together in 3 rows containing 3 blocks as shown in the assembly diagram.

6 | Your pillow top is now complete. Quilt if desired.

7 | Complete your pillow using the instructions at the end of the chapter.

Assembly Diagram

▲ **Home Run,** 21" (53.3cm)

❖ Finished pillow measures 24" (61cm) square

Mrs. Bannister's Stars

The block in this design can be made with as few as four fabrics or with as many as you'd like. The corners can be varied from block to block. You can set them with sashing or alternate plain blocks, but I like them set edge to edge.

Because the finished block measures 12" (30.5cm), you can easily multiply this to make any size quilt you'd like.

▼ MATERIALS & SUPPLIES

⅓ yd. (30cm) of colored fabric in a variety of spots, stripes, prints, etc. (fat sixteenths work well or use fabric from your stash)

Four ¼ yd. (23cm) cuts for block backgrounds

¼ yd. (23cm) of dark contrast fabric

¾ yd. (68cm) fabric for backing

¾ yd. (68cm) fabric for lining

¾ yd. (68cm) square of batting

24" (61cm) zipper

Sewing machine

Zipper foot

Matching cotton thread for sewing

Quilting thread (optional)

Template plastic

General sewing notions (pins, scissors, tape measure, etc.)

Templates T22, T23, T24, T24 REVERSE, T25 and T25 REVERSE (on pattern sheet 1)

Cutting Instructions

Finished block measures 12" (30.5cm).

For each block, cut:

4 of template T22 from colored fabric (16 total)

4 of template T23 from colored fabric (16 total)

4 of template T24 from colored fabric (16 total)

4 of template T24 REVERSE from dark fabric (16 total)

4 of template T25 from colored fabric (16 total)

4 of template T25 REVERSE from colored fabric (16 total)

Block assembly

1 | Stitch a T24 piece to the right side of a T22 piece (*Figure 1*).

FIGURE 1

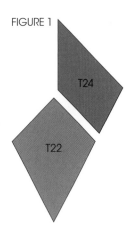

2 | Stitch a T24 REVERSE piece to the other side of the unit just sewn so it joins both the T22 and T24 pieces (*Figure 2*). Make 4 units.

3 | Stitch a T23 piece to the right side of a previously made unit (*Figure 3*). Repeat with all 4 units.

4 | Stitch the units made in step 3 together in pairs (*Figure 4*).

5 | Stitch the pairs made in step 4 together across the center seam (*Figure 5*).

FIGURE 4

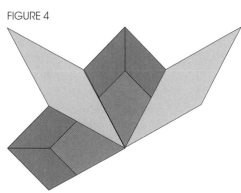

FIGURE 5

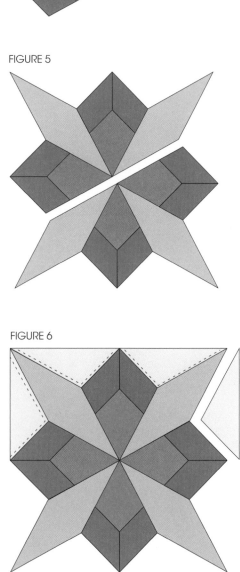

FIGURE 2

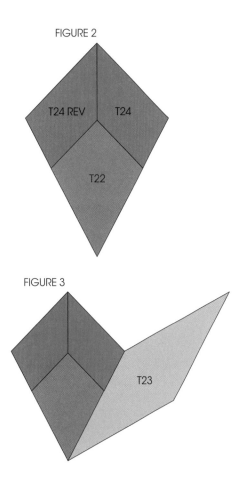

T24 REV   T24

T22

FIGURE 3

T23

FIGURE 6

6 | Insert T25 and T25 REVERSE pieces around the edge of the block. This can be done in a continuous seam (*Figure 6*).

7 | To make the pillow front, stitch 4 finished blocks together (*Figure 7*).

8 | Your pillow top is now complete. Finish the pillow according to the instructions at the end of the chapter.

   If you decide to make a quilt, join the blocks into rows, then join the rows together.

FIGURE 7

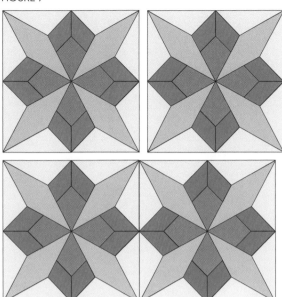

▲ **Mrs. Bannister's Stars,** 24" (61cm)

Clam Bake

I have always loved the Clam Shell pattern. Some wonderful versions have been made over the years, and I hope mine will only add to the great designs I've seen.

I've divided most of the clams into three parts, but I've added a few solid clams along the way to provided visual interest and a place for the eye to rest. You could try alternating rows of pieced clams with full clams for a different look. It would also be quicker to make!

I have hand pieced this pillow, but it would be easy to machine stitch because the curves are quite gentle.

▼ MATERIALS & SUPPLIES

⅝ yd. (57cm) in total of a variety of fabric (fat sixteenths work well)

¼ yd. (23cm) fabric for borders

⅝ yd. (57cm) fabric for backing

20" (51cm) zipper

Sewing machine

¼" (6mm) sewing machine foot

Zipper foot

Matching cotton thread for sewing

Aurifil 12-weight thread for hand quilting

Rotary cutter

Cutting mat

Ruler

General sewing notions (pins, scissors, tape measure, etc.)

Template plastic

Templates T36, T37, T38, T39, T40, T41, T42 and T43 (on pattern sheet 1)

This pillow is hand pieced. Draw your stitching line around the templates, then add a ¼" (6mm) seam allowance. Rotary cutting instructions (strips) include a ¼" (6mm) seam allowance.

Cutting Instructions

For each pieced clam, cut:
   1 from template T36 (18 total)
   1 from template T37 (18 total)
   1 from template T38 (18 total)

Make 18 pieced clams.

For the solid clams, cut:
   2 from template T39

For the half clams (at sides), cut:
   T40, T41 and T42 to make 4 half clams for the left side

   T40, T41 and T42 in reverse to make 3 half clams for the right side

   T40, T41 and T42 combined for a solid clam

For the top and bottom edges, cut:
   4 from template T43 (for top)

   3 from template T36

   3 from template T37

Note: *The T36 and T37 templates create the 3 incomplete clams across the bottom of the pillow.*

Pillow Assembly

1 | Mark the centers of the pieces. Pin at each end and in the center (*Figure 1*). Stitch. (You might find it easier to have the concave edge facing you when you stitch.)

Note: *Some people find stitching curves difficult, but remember that there's always a degree of bias present in curves. Because of this bias stretch, you have the ability to make things fit. You're the boss!*

2 | Stitch the pieced clam shells (18 in total) and the half shells for the edges. Remember to make 4 half shells for the left side and 3 reversed for the right side. Also cut 1 half clam from a solid fabric.

3 | Make the 3 incomplete clams for the bottom edge.

4 | Stitch the rows together on the diagonal (*Figure 2*). Once your rows are complete, the top of your panel will look like the image shown in Figure 3.

5 | Insert the 4 T43 pieces (*Figure 3*).

6 | Press the pillow top, then trim the sides and the bottom edge to square it off.

7 | Add a small outer border as follows:
    Cut 2 strips 2½" × 16½" (6.4cm × 41.9cm) and stitch them to each side.
    Cut 2 strips 2½" × 22½" (6.4cm × 57.2cm) and stitch to the top and bottom.

8 | Your clam shell panel is now complete. Finish the pillow using the instructions at the end of the chapter.

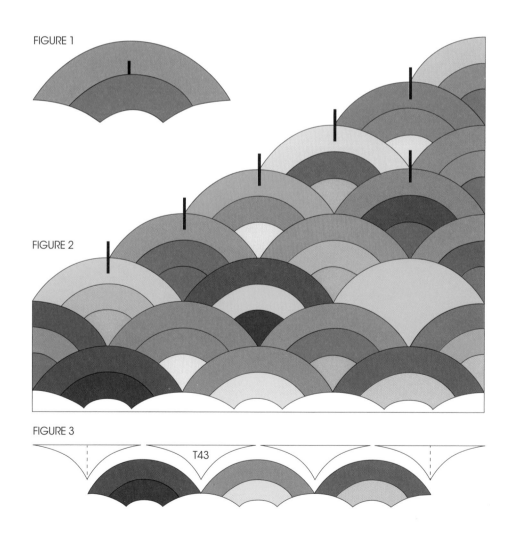

FIGURE 1

FIGURE 2

FIGURE 3

T43

Quilting

9 | If desired, quilt your pillow before following the final assembly instruction. I hand quilted this project with Aurifil 12-weight thread by following the top of each clam.

-----------------**MAKE IT A QUILT**

If you want to create a larger project, just keep making clam shells! The top and bottom are the same. You simply need to cut more pieces.

▲ **Clam Bake,** 20" × 22" (50.8cm × 55.9cm)

Small Wonders

❖ Finished cushion measures 21" (53.3cm) square

Made of little 3" (7.6cm) blocks, this pillow design would also make a divine crib quilt.

Five different blocks are included in this design, but you could choose to make any one block and repeat it as often as you wish.

▼ MATERIALS & SUPPLIES

½ yd. (46cm) total of a wide variety of fabrics (fat sixteenths work well, or use up fabrics from your stash); include fabrics for contrast and background

4 fabrics from which you can cut 22" × 2" (55.9cm × 5.1cm) strips for borders

⅝ yd. (57cm) fabric for backing

22" (56cm) square of batting (if you choose to quilt)

⅝ yd. (57cm) fabric for lining

20" (51cm) zipper

Sewing machine

¼" (6mm) sewing machine foot

Zipper foot

Matching cotton thread

Quilting thread (optional)

Rotary cutter

Cutting mat

Ruler

General sewing notions (pins, scissors, tape measure, etc.)

A ¼" (6mm) seam allowance is included in all cutting instructions.

Make 9 blocks in total.

This project uses two blocks each of Square in a Square, Hearts, 9 Patch and Friendship Star, and one Shoo Fly block.

Square in a Square Block
Finished blocks measure 3" (7.6cm).

Make 2 blocks total.

From your fabrics, cut:
   1 square at 3½" (8.9cm) (2 total)
   4 squares at 2" (5.1cm) (8 total)

BLOCK ASSEMBLY
1 | Draw a diagonal line down the center of the 2" (5.1cm) squares. Be sure to draw on the wrong side of the fabric.

2 | Place these 2 squares on diagonally opposite corners of the 3½" (8.9cm) square with right sides together (*Figure 1*).

3 | Stitch on the drawn line. Cut off the corners, leaving a ¼" (6mm) seam allowance (as shown in Figure 2 on page 98).

FIGURE 1

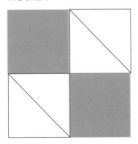

4 | Press to complete the corner. Repeat with the remaining corners (*Figure 3*).

Shoo Fly Block

Finished block measures 3" (7.6cm).

Make 1 block total.

From your fabrics, cut:

2 squares at 1⅞" (4.8cm) from background fabric

2 squares at 1⅞" (4.8cm) from colored fabrics

5 squares at 1½" (3.8cm) (4 from any fabric and

1 from a contrast fabric)

BLOCK ASSEMBLY

5 | Place a 1⅞" (4.8cm) square of background fabric and a 1⅞" (4.8cm) square of colored fabric together with right sides facing.

6 | Draw a diagonal line (solid line in Figure 4) from corner to corner on the back of the top square, then stitch on each side of this line with a ¼" (6mm) seam allowance (dashed lines in Figure 4).

7 | Cut on the drawn line, then open the new units and press the seam allowances toward the darker fabric.

8 | Repeat with the remaining 1⅞" (4.8cm) squares. This will make a total of 4 half-square triangles.

9 | Sew the blocks together as shown in Figure 5.

FIGURE 2

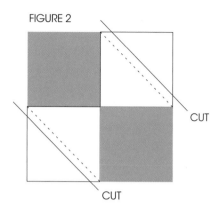

CUT

CUT

FIGURE 3

FIGURE 4

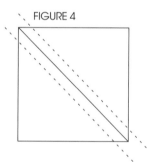

FIGURE 5

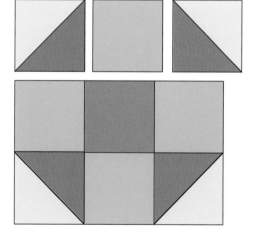

Nine-Patch Block

Finished blocks measure 3" (7.6cm).

Make 2 blocks total.

From your fabrics, cut:

9 squares at 1½" (3.8cm) (*Figure 6*) (8 total)

or

4 squares each from 2 contrasting fabrics (8 total)

1 square for the center 1½" (3.8cm) (*Figure 7*) (2 total)

BLOCK ASSEMBLY

10 | Stitch together the squares as shown in Figures 6 and 7.

Friendship Star Block

Finished blocks measure 3" (7.6cm).

Make 2 blocks total.

From your fabrics, cut:

Cut 4 squares at 1½" (3.8cm) from background fabric (8 total)

Cut 2 squares at 1⅞" (4.8cm) from background fabric (8 total)

Cut 2 squares at 1⅞" (4.8cm) from contrast fabric (8 total)

Cut 1 square at 1½" (3.8cm) from contrast fabric (8 total)

BLOCK ASSEMBLY

11 | Place a 1⅞" (4.8cm) square of background fabric and a 1⅞" (4.8cm) square of contrast fabric together with the right sides facing. Draw a diagonal line (solid line in Figure 8) on the background fabric and stitch with a ¼" (6mm) seam allowance (dashed lines in Figure 8) on each side of the line.

12 | Cut on the drawn line, open the units and press the seam allowances toward the darker fabric (*Figure 8*).

13 | Repeat with the remaining squares to make a total of 4 half-square triangles.

14 | Stitch the blocks together as shown in Figure 9 on page 100.

FIGURE 6

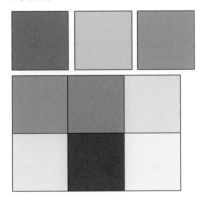

FIGURE 7

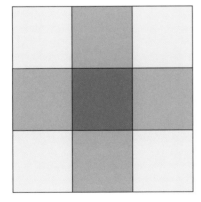

FIGURE 8

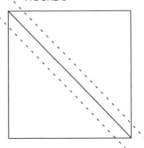

Heart Block

Finished blocks measure 3" (7.6cm).

Make 2 blocks total.

From your fabrics, cut:

2 squares at 2" (5.1cm) from contrast fabric (4 total)

4 squares at 1¼" (3.2cm) from background fabric (8 total)

1 square at 2⅜" (6cm) from background fabric (2 total)

1 square at 2⅜" (6cm) from contrast fabric (2 total)

BLOCK ASSEMBLY

15 | Draw diagonal lines on the wrong sides of the four 1¼" (3.2cm) background squares.

16 | Place one of these background squares in the corner of a 2" (5.1cm) contrast square (*Figure 10*).

17 | Stitch on the drawn line (shown as dashed in Figure 10). Trim off the corner, leaving a ¼" (6mm) seam allowance. Press the corner, then repeat on the opposite corner (*Figure 11*).
　　Make 2 units.

FIGURE 9

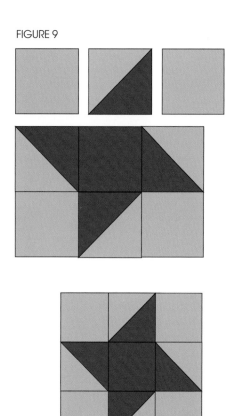

FIGURE 10

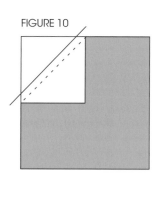

FIGURE 11

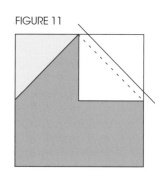

18 | Place a 2⅜" (6cm) square of background fabric and a 2⅜" (6cm) square of contrast fabric with right sides together.

19 | Draw diagonal lines and stitch with a ¼" (6mm) seam allowance on each side of the line.

20 | Cut on the drawn line. Open the unit and press the seam allowances toward the darker fabric.

21 | Stitch the block together as shown in Figure 12.

Add Log Cabin Edges
For each block, cut:
   1 strip at 1½" x 3½" (3.8cm × 8.9cm) (9 total)

   2 strips at 1½" x 4½" (3.8cm × 11.4cm) (18 total)

   2 strips at 1½" x 5½" (3.8cm × 14cm) (18 total)

   1 strip at 1½" x 6½" (3.8cm × 16.5cm) (9 total)

ASSEMBLY
22 | Stitch the strips as shown in Figure 13. Remember to press the seam allowances toward the outside of the block as you go.

   The blocks will now measure 6½" (16.5cm) including seam allowance.

23 | Stitch the blocks together in 3 rows of 3 blocks (*Figure 14*).

FIGURE 12

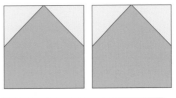
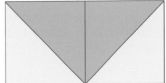

FIGURE 13

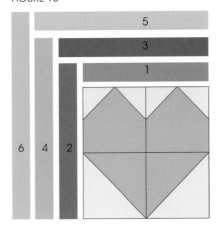

FIGURE 14

Add a Border

From fabric, cut:

1 strip at 2" × 18½" (5.1cm × 47cm)

2 strips 2" × 20" (5.1cm × 50.8cm)

1 strip 2" × 21½" (5.1cm × 54.6cm)

ASSEMBLY

24 | Stitch the strips to the pillow top as shown in Figure 15.

25 | Your pillow top is now complete. Quilt, if desired, and finish the pillow according to the instructions at the end of the chapter. You can also make more blocks to expand the design into a quilt.

FIGURE 15

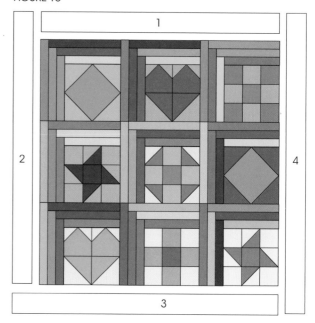

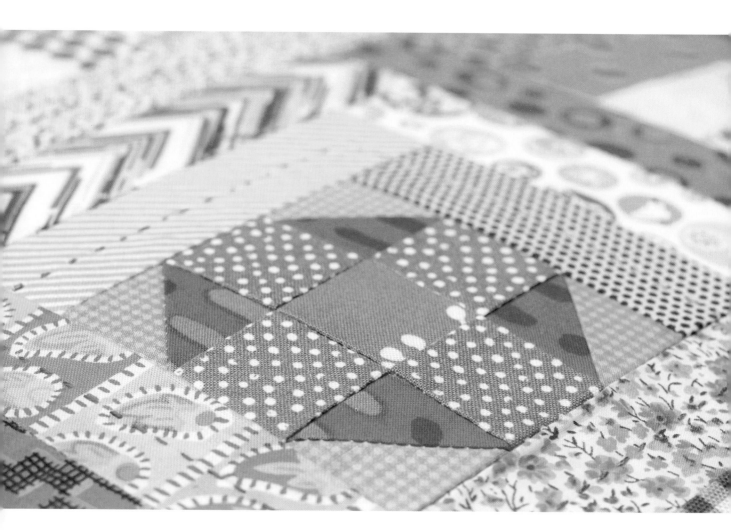

▲ **Small Wonders,** 21" (53.3cm)

Pillow Assembly

1 | Measure your front panel and cut your chosen backing fabric to match the height plus an additional 2"–3" (5.1cm–7.6cm) added to the length measurement.

2 | Cut this panel into 2 pieces (*Figure 1*) (I cut mine off-center because I like the effect).

3 | Cut a strip 2" (5.1cm) by the pillow's height measurement. This can be from the same fabric as the backing or a contrasting fabric if desired. Your zipper should also be approximately this measurement or slightly smaller.

4 | Fold the 2" (5.1cm) strip in half lengthwise with the wrong sides together. Press.

5 | Place the large rectangle with the right side facing you. Lay the folded strip with the cut edges along the edge of the rectangle, then place the zipper wrong-side up on the edge of the strip with the tab at the bottom. Align the edges and, with a zipper foot attached to your machine, stitch close to the teeth on your zipper (*Figure 2*).

6 | Flip the zipper and the folded strip over. Press.

FIGURE 1

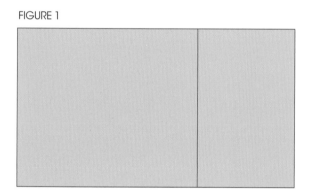

FIGURE 2

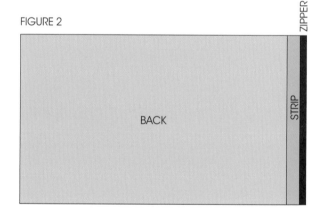

FIGURE 3

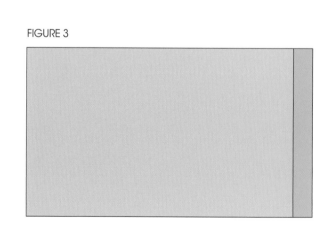

7 | The seam will face the large rectangle. The zipper should now sit under the folded strip (*Figure 3*).

8 | Place the smaller rectangle and the zipper together with right sides facing. Stitch close to the zipper teeth. Make sure the raw edge of the rectangle is aligned with the zipper tape edge and the folded strip covering is out of the way. Press the seams toward the rectangle. Your zipper should be lying flat (hidden) beneath the folded strip.

9 | With the right side of the pillow back facing up, lay the pillow front on top with right sides together. Remember to leave the zipper open 3"–4" (7.6cm–10.2cm) so you can turn your pillow right-side out after sewing.

10 | Using a ¼" (6mm) seam allowance, stitch around the 4 sides. Trim the excess from the backing if necessary.

11 | Turn the pillow cover right-side out through the open zipper. Press well and topstitch close to the edge, if desired.

Your pillow cover is now complete! Insert a pillow form or stuff with polyester filling to finish.

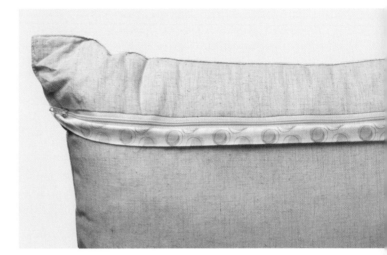

---------------------------**FINISHING TIP**
Another finishing option is to bind the edge of the pillow as you would bind a quilt. This gives the pillow an effect similar to piping.

Cut binding strips a little narrower than you normally would for a quilt (I suggest 1½"–2" [3.8cm–5.1cm]), depending on the size of your pillow. Smaller pillows will need narrower binding to appear properly balanced and proportioned.

Appendix A: Before You Begin

Designing Quilts and Choosing Fabrics

Creating a design and selecting the fabrics is, without a doubt, my favorite part of any project. Being surrounded by wonderful fabric hues warms me to the very core.

Sometimes, however, the enormous selection of available choices can be daunting. If you find yourself worrying about what colors to put together, take a look at Mother Nature and observe her rules: She has none. Nature does not plan which flowers bloom next to one another or which trees, with their various greens, stand tall and proud side by side.

In the past, quilting was born of necessity, and quilts were constructed from available materials. Today we have the most incredible supply of gorgeous and varied textiles, but we restrict ourselves with rules that were made up over time.

Personally, I find the color wheel confusing, and if you listen carefully to people who preach the virtue of colors remaining grouped together in specific arrangements or families, you'll ultimately hear that all colors work together.

The most important question when choosing your fabrics is do you like the color combination you have chosen? This is what matters, and if the answer is yes, then begin your work proudly.

I believe we all see color a little differently, and what works for one person might not work for another, and that's okay.

In this section, I discuss some of the things that work for me, but I'm in no way saying that these are the correct or only approaches.

Be brave. Experiment and play with different options, stretch your boundaries and, most of all, have fun.

THINK OUTSIDE THE BOX

Many years ago, I heard the delightful Freddy Moran say that red is a neutral, and that ten fabrics don't work, but one hundred or more do.

I have thought about these statements over the years, and I have repeated both to many quilters.

Think about red as a background or neutral. What color doesn't work with red?

Orange and red: Great
Green and red: Christmas
Hot pink and red: Wonderful
Purple and red: Striking
Aqua and red: Perfect
Black, white and red: Fantastic
And the list goes on and on....

Including many fabrics in one project has always been my passion. If you have only four to six fabrics in your quilt, you have to be much more disciplined and coordinated with your approach.

If you have one hundred or more fabrics, as I often do, you'll be amazed at how easily they work together.

WHAT I USE AND WHAT I DO

I use reproduction fabrics next to brights, florals, checks, geometrics and stripes.

I never use an entire range of fabrics, because I find they blend too well and are too perfectly color matched. To me, this creates a flat and uninteresting effect.

I love Japanese fabrics for their wacky and unusual combinations.

I use different weights of fabrics, such as linens, cottons and voiles in one project.

I love textured fabrics.

I use what I love and what I think looks good together.

> **TIP**---------------------------------
> If you're using a fabric that moves or stretches too much, a simple trick is to give it a good douse of spray starch. This will stabilize it and make cutting and stitching a little easier.

ABOUT BACKGROUND FABRICS

When choosing background fabrics, consider the following:

- Mix whites, creams and light grays with beiges and taupes for a vintage feel.
- Strong, dark backgrounds make colors pop.
- Patterned fabrics (such as text prints) make wonderful backgrounds and add visual interest.

POINTS TO CONSIDER WHEN GATHERING AND PREPARING FABRICS

BUILDING A FABRIC LIBRARY, AKA YOUR STASH

You need a good stash to make truly wonderful scrappy quilts.

For the majority of my feature fabrics, I usually purchase 12" (30.5cm) cuts.

If you love something and think you could use it for a border, purchase 3 yards (2.7m).

I purchase most backgrounds and neutrals in ½ yard (0.5m) to 1 yard (0.9m) cuts.

Don't be afraid to mix many different backgrounds in one project or to purchase strong prints with the purpose of using them as a background.

Make sure you have an eclectic mix of florals, geometrics, stripes and dots in a wide color range in your stash. Be sure to have both large- and small-scale prints to create variety.

Look for fabric designs that will be especially suited to fussy cutting. You will need to purchase larger quantities of these.

Be aware of the wrong side of the fabric as well. Sometimes both sides yield wonderful results.

When at the fabric store, don't dismiss fabrics on the shelf at first glance. You can only see a slim portion of the print on the bolt, and this will not fully showcase its hidden beauty. Take the bolt down and unroll some of the fabric so you can see the entire design.

NATURAL LIGHTING

Natural lighting always shows the true colors in a print. The type of lighting and bulb color in a shop or in your work space can influence and change hues.

THREAD COUNT AND QUALITY

Today, most fabrics manufactured for the quilting industry are good quality, but thread count still needs some discussion. The term "thread count" refers to the number of threads woven together in one square inch (2.5cm) of fabric. The threads are counted in both directions. For instance, one hundred threads lengthwise (warp) and one hundred threads widthwise (weft) would be a thread count of two hundred.

If the thread count is too high, the fabric becomes difficult for a needle to pierce, which is especially problematic when hand sewing. If the thread count is too low, however, the fabric will fray easily and will not be suitable for projects such as needle-turn appliqué.

COLOR FASTNESS

I rarely wash my fabrics, but if I'm concerned about color migration, I test a small piece of the fabric. I begin by wetting it thoroughly, then I place it to dry on a white paper towel. If there is any sign of color bleeding from the fabric to the paper towel, I wash all of the fabrics for the project.

Prewash fabrics in the same way you will wash the finished quilt. Use a chlorine-free detergent and wash on a delicate cycle.

STORING YOUR FABRIC STASH

Depending on the amount of fabric you have purchased, your storage needs will vary greatly.

I use storage boxes with pullout drawers and group my fabrics by color. That way, if I need to add just of touch of violet, I can select the correct drawer and browse the available choices.

There are dozens of ways to store your stash, however, depending on your available space and organizational preferences. I've found that browsing online yields many great recommendations for stash management.

CONTRAST AND VALUE (OR TONE)

We all fall into the trap of purchasing only our favorite fabrics. In my experience, these fabrics tend to be medium values, which do not allow for much variety in selection.

You need to have a range of values, from lights to darks, but be aware that contrast also depends on what fabrics sit next to one another. Red will read as a dark when next to white, but it can read as a light or medium in a quilt with a black or dark base.

Pattern and print size also need to vary to add movement and interest. If you are concerned when making your quilt, stand back and look at it from a distance. This is where a design wall is a handy tool.

Taking a photograph or looking through a reducing lens (the opposite of a magnifying glass) will also help to pinpoint areas of your quilt that stand out or get lost.

BACKINGS

I usually purchase 5–6 yards (4.6–5.5m) for the backs of my quilts. Some people piece their backs, which is also an acceptable approach. However, because I usually hand quilt, I prefer not to have excess seams to quilt through.

I am fond of bold backs, but I always consider what color thread I plan to quilt with before deciding on the backing.

Most people find it harder to get a perfect quilting stitch on the back of their quilt. Purchasing a fabric pattern and color that will complement your quilt top as well as your chosen quilting thread color can assist in masking or hiding these little imperfections.

I love quilting with voile or lawn as a backing. The feeling when it's finished is soft and oh-so-cuddly.

When choosing your backing fabric, give the fabric a small test with a needle to make sure it's easy to stitch through. This is especially important when hand quilting. As previously mentioned, some fabrics with higher thread counts can be difficult to stitch through.

BINDING

Purchasing the right binding fabric is important because the binding acts as a frame for your quilt top. A fabric that is too bold will draw your eye to the outside of the quilt, but a binding that is not bold enough will disappear into the edge. Choosing a shade lighter or darker than your quilt top can make all the difference.

I rarely choose my binding before my quilt is quilted. Once the quilting is finished, I audition several fabrics before making a decision. To do this, I fold the fabric over the edge of the quilt to see if it will work with my finished design. Stripes often look wonderful when cut on the straight grain or on the bias.

CHOOSING FABRICS FOR A PARTICULAR PROJECT

If you aren't sure how to get started, choose just one fabric that you adore. This can be your jumping-off point, and it will help you draw other prints and patterns into the mix. It's usually best if you start with a fabric that has several colors in the pattern and a bold print focus.

When you're ready to head to your local quilt shop, give yourself plenty of time to choose. It can take quite a while, and you don't want to be rushed to make a decision.

As you progress through the selection process, don't be surprised if your original fabric becomes lost in your take-home bundle. That's fine. It was just a way to get the ideas flowing.

You might purchase all the fabrics you need at once or, like I do, leave a little wiggle room. As you get into the design process, it will become obvious if you need to add more color, contrast or pattern to the project.

Quilts don't have to have huge contrast to look beautiful. Low-contrast quilts can be gorgeous as well. Some quilts look stunning when made with just two colors. Many quilts from the past used this formula.

Keep in mind that you can still make a low-contrast quilt using many fabrics. For instance, a red-and-white quilt can be made using reds, pinks, whites and beiges. This selection of colors gives the quilt a vintage feel as well.

Equipment

Many wonderful tools and gadgets on the market are useful and fun. Beginners are often overwhelmed by the selection. Some items may be a little costly, but my recommendation is to

--------------------------------DESIGN WALLS

While making a quilt a few years ago, I lost my way. I was in over my head and couldn't see the direction I needed the design to go.

Later, while at a quilting retreat, another attendee had a portable design wall. She placed my quilt blocks up on the wall, and my perspective changed immediately!

With a design wall, you can audition fabrics, check colors and values in borders or sashings, or lay out your quilt blocks to get an even distribution of pattern, value and color. ✎

If you have the luxury of space, you can mount a permanent design wall in your studio. If not, there are many portable versions on the market for purchase. Some have collapsible frames, and some have eyelets that you can hang from picture hooks or nails.

You can also create your own design wall using basic materials. Attach batting or flannel to a stiff backing, such as corkboard or foam core board. Both of these backing materials will allow you to use pins, which can be useful when your blocks or quilt tops become a little heavier. For single blocks or smaller quilt assemblies, however, the fabric will naturally adhere to the batting or flannel without the use of pins.

Creating a design wall is definitely worth the effort, and it will give you an excellent way to view and arrange your blocks before sewing them together.

buy smart and buy the best quality possible. If you do, these items will last for many years to come.

Your local quilt shop is a great place to begin, and the store's staff should be able to help you decide what's most important. In addition, here are some suggestions that will serve you well:

GENERAL EQUIPMENT

Pins: Good-quality fine pins are essential. Do not use blunt or bent pens, as this could damage your fabric or misalign your piecing.

Pencils and markers: Permanent fine-line marking pens are excellent for marking templates, because the ink will not rub off.

On fabrics, I mark with a 2B lead pencil. I prefer a 0.7mm mechanical pencil because the lead stays sharp and the line is fine and accurate. If I need to use an alternate color to mark fabric, I use a chalk or ceramic lead in a contrasting color.

Template plastic: This see-through plastic is used to make templates for any quilting shape you might need. You can purchase either plain sheets or sheets with a ¼" (6mm) printed grid.

Cardboard may also be used to make templates; however, you won't be able to see through it. This won't be as useful as the translucent plastic if you need to fussy cut your fabric.

Scissors: Buy the best-quality scissors you can afford. Poor-quality scissors will dull very quickly and damage your fabric. Also, be sure to use your fabric scissors with fabric only. Cutting paper or plastic will dull or nick the blades.

For quilting, scissors with shorter blades—about 5"–7" (12.7cm–17.8cm)—are better than large dressmakers shears. They provide more control and are easier to manage when cutting small shapes. My scissors have a finely serrated blade that grips the fabric and prevents slippage, especially when cutting fine voile or lawn.

You should also keep a pair of not-so-special scissors that can be used for cutting plastic and paper. Again, don't be tempted to use your fabric-cutting scissors for this purpose.

Thread: Choose a 100% cotton thread for both machine and hand piecing. Polyester threads are much stronger and, over time, could cut through the cotton fabrics in your quilt.

I prefer to hand sew with 40- or 50-weight thread. These are standard weights when piecing, but try various thread weights to see what works best for you and gives you the results you desire.

When machine stitching, some machines perform better when using a particular thread. Check your manual if you're uncertain what your machine requires.

For general hand piecing or machine piecing, I recommend using a neutral thread color such as white, gray or taupe, depending on the colors in your quilt.

Iron: An iron is essential for pressing seams into nice, straight lines that are easy to line up and quilt over.

Tape measure: A good tape measure is a handy item to have for any sewing endeavor. Be sure your tape measure is not stretched out of shape before using it.

Notepad: A notepad is essential for jotting down measurements and making notes about changes or decisions you've made for your quilt.

Resealable plastic bags: Plastic bags are perfect for storing anything and everything! You can buy smaller resealable bags in the jewelry department of most craft shops, or you can use regular sandwich or snack bags from your local grocer. Pint- or quart-sized (milliliters or liters) bags are great for storing color-sorted scraps.

FOR MACHINE PIECING

Sewing machine: Some machines have lots of bells and whistles but may be of lesser quality for the price. You need to consider what features you will use and purchase the best-quality machine you can afford. Some handy features for quilt making include the following:
- A ¼" (6mm) presser foot or the ability to move the needle position to make it stitch ¼" (6mm) from the edge of your regular presser foot
- A needle-up and needle-down position
- A walking foot or dual feed dogs
- Retractable feed dogs

Rotary cutter: A 45mm rotary cutter is a standard size for general quilting and easy to locate at any craft store. Ergonomic rotary cutters are more comfortable and usually have an automatic safety guard, but buy whatever style you prefer.

Self-healing cutting mat: An 18" × 24" (45.7cm × 61cm) cutting mat is a midsize board large enough to cut almost everything but still easy to fit on a table or carry to class. A self-healing mat is important because ridges caused by a rotary cutter on a nonhealing mat might cause your fabric to snag or your cutter to deviate from a straight line.

Grid ruler: A 12½" × 6½" (31.8cm × 16.5cm) ruler is the best size to use when quilting. Other sizes can be added when you need them, but this standard ruler will be able to handle most projects.

FOR HAND PIECING

Sandpaper boards: Sandpaper boards grip your fabric as you trace around templates, and they prevent distortion as your pencil or chalk moves over the fabric's surface. You should be able to purchase a sandpaper board at any craft or quilt shop, but if you are having difficulty finding one, a sheet of fine-grade sandpaper will work just as effectively.

Needles: I prefer to use milliner (or straw) needles in size 10 or 11 for piecing, but any sharp needle will work just as well, provided you find it easy to use.

¼" (6mm) seam marker: A seam wheel or wonder wheel allows you to add seam allowances around templates and curves easily. A ¼" (6mm) seam marking ruler will also work.

Thimbles: Thimbles take time to get used to, but once you do, they're invaluable. There are many shapes, sizes and materials on the market, including metal, leather and silicone. Explore your options and get one that's comfortable on your finger and suits your stitching method. Thimbles are an extremely personal item, so get one that works for you.

Finger protectors/finger cots: I find a finger cot or rubber finger stall very useful. I wear it on my index finger, next to the thimble on my middle finger. It acts as a needle grabber and reduces the strain on my thumb joint.

There are also a number of stick-on disks that can be used to prevent sore spots on your fingers.

FOR NEEDLE-TURN APPLIQUÉ

Small appliqué pins: These pins are just the right size for holding your appliqué designs onto the quilt.

Appliqué glue: This water-soluble glue holds your appliqué in place while you sew. The glue will disappear after the first quilt wash.

Thread: 50-weight thread is best for needle-turn appliqué, and it's available in a wide range of colors.

Needles: Size 11 milliner (straw) needles work well for appliqué.

Bias tape maker: Bias tape makes creating appliqué stems a breeze. Use the bias tape maker to make a large quantity of tape at once, then store it wrapped around an empty plastic wrap roll (cardboard tube) and have it on hand anytime you need it.

Mylar circle template: If your appliqué has a lot of circular shapes, this is a wonderful tool. The Mylar is heat resistant, so you can press your fabric against the template with an iron for a perfect shape.

Markers: 2B lead pencils and silver gel pens are probably the only two markers you will require, but many types of markers are available.

Templates: Create appliqué templates using template plastic, cardboard, freezer paper or plain paper. Whatever works best for you will do the trick.

FOR HAND QUILTING

Thread: When hand quilting, you can use a waxed thread specifically prepared for this purpose (it's thicker than the thread used for piecing). I quilt with a Perle 8- or 12-weight thread, which makes a bolder stitch. I find this thread quicker and easier to use because you quilt with a larger stitch, and it creates a beautiful effect on the finished quilt.

Hoops: There are many different types of quilting hoops on the market: circular, square, hand-held and stand-alone frames. Choose a size and shape that works for you, or you can choose to lap quilt, which does not involve a hoop at all (lap quilting is my favorite way to hand quilt).

Needles: Needle selection will vary depending on the method of hand quilting you choose. If you use the rocking method or prefer stab quilting, use shorter needles. If you use thicker thread, such as perle thread, try crewel or chenille needles.

Thimbles: A good thimble is even more important in hand quilting than it is in hand piecing. Find one that works for your style of quilting, and you'll discover it's absolutely invaluable.

FOR MACHINE QUILTING

Thread: Machine quilting thread is available in a wide range of colors. It's a heavier weight than regular and piecing thread, and it is not waxed. Do not use a waxed hand-quilting thread in your sewing machine.

Walking foot: A walking foot is essential for straight-line quilting with your machine. It creates a dual feed dog system that allows the multiple layers of your quilt to pass through the machine easily and without slippage. If your sewing machine comes with a built-in dual feed dog system, you will not need a walking foot.

Free-motion quilting foot: Many sewing machines come with an optional free-motion quilting foot. The spring in this foot allows you to move your quilt in any direction you choose, giving you free reign to quilt any shape you desire. When using this foot, be sure to lower your feed dogs.

Hand Piecing

Although much slower than machine piecing, hand piecing is relaxing, portable and satisfying. Although many patterns lend themselves to the ease of machine stitching, others are more accurately worked by hand. Some traditional designs, especially those with curved seams, are difficult to stitch by machine and are almost always hand sewn.

MAKING TEMPLATES

Making templates is the first step in making your quilt after you have decided on a design.

Templates for hand piecing do not traditionally have the seam allowance included, but this is something you must check for each pattern.

Draw the individual elements onto template plastic using your fine-tip black permanent marker. Carefully cut out the template and remember that the drawn line is the outside edge of your template.

Label each individual shape with the corresponding letter or number and grainline on your pattern, if appropriate (*Figure 1*). I also like to write the name of the block or quilt and the size of the block on each template.

MARKING AND CUTTING FABRIC

Lay your chosen fabric wrong-side up on a sandpaper board. Place your template on the fabric, aligning grain lines or capturing the design of the fabric as desired. Trace around the template with a visible pencil or marking tool. Be careful not to pull or stretch the fabric. Remove the template and, with your ¼" (6mm) ruler, draw your seam allowance around the perimeter of the shape (*Figure 2*).

This step is important because your first drawn line will be the stitching line you follow when sewing. If the template were to have the seam allowance included, you would not know where your stitching line was located, which would probably result in incorrect finished sizes.

Separate your cut shapes into groups that are easily identifiable. I typically use resealable plastic bags to store my cut shapes (each set of shapes in a separate bag with the template).

FIGURE 1

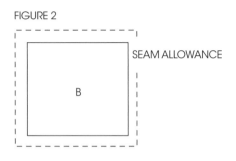

FIGURE 2

SEAM ALLOWANCE

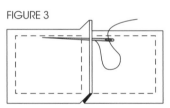

FIGURE 3

HAND SEWING YOUR PATCHWORK

Remember, accurate seam allowances are a must for accurate patchwork.

When constructing blocks, keep in mind the basic principles of combining smaller pieces to larger units, combining larger units into rows or sections, and joining sections into complete blocks.

Join pieces with pins, match marked sewing lines and sew with a running stitch from seamline to seamline, not edge to edge (*Figure 3*).

As you sew, check to be sure your stitching is staying on the lines. Make a backstitch every 1" (2.5cm) or so to reinforce and strengthen the seam. Secure corners with an extra backstitch.

When you cross the seam allowances of previously joined smaller units, make a backstitch just before and just after you cross over. Leave the seams free rather than stitching them down.

Needle-Turn Appliqué

The term "appliqué" refers to the process of layering one fabric over another and stitching the top fabric to the background fabric. Needle turn is a method in which the seams are turned under with the tip of the needle just ahead of the section being stitched.

There are many materials available for making appliqué templates, including paper, freezer paper and template plastic. I typically use template plastic, but feel free to use whatever material you prefer.

MAKING THE TEMPLATES

Trace your design onto the plastic using a fine-tip permanent black marker.

Label each piece with the block number and template label. For example, "block 1, template T1."

Cut on the drawn line. Be careful to cut as accurately as possible.

CUTTING OUT THE APPLIQUÉ

Lay your chosen fabric right-side up on a sandpaper board. Using a fine-tip marker, trace around the template on the right side of the fabric.

Cut out the shape, adding approximately a ⅛" (3.2mm) seam allowance from the traced line.

SEWING THE APPLIQUÉ

Pin the appliqué pieces in place.

I do not usually mark my background but, if you prefer, lightly mark the placement diagram on your background fabric using a light box.

Remember to layer the pieces. The shapes in the background are sewn before the shapes in the foreground. For instance, stems must be sewn first because the flowers will overlap the raw edges.

Give the appliqué shape a light finger press along the seam allowance lines. This helps when turning under the edges.

Begin stitching on a fairly straight portion of the shape, not at a point. The point will be much easier to control if the seam leading to the point is already secured.

Bring your knotted thread up from the back of your appliqué shape and through a point on the marked line (do not come through the background because you will not be able to tuck your seam allowance under).

With the point of your needle, turn the seam allowance under until the marked line is not visible (*Figure 4*).

You will need to turn the fabric in front of your stitching under approximately ½"–¾" (1.3cm–1.9cm) and hold it down with the thumb of your non-stitching hand.

Use a blind stitch and a thread color that matches the appliqué, not the background fabric. I use cotton thread, but some people prefer silk thread.

Place your stitch directly into the background fabric, next to the stitch in the appliqué and as close to the edge as possible (*Figure 5*). Stitches should be ¹⁄₁₆" (2mm) apart or closer.

TIPS

Try using an ultra-fine permanent marker or silver gel pen to draw appliqué shapes on your fabric. The seam allowance will be turned under when you sew, and the drawn lines will not be visible.

For easy identification, store cut appliqué shapes with their corresponding templates in resealable plastic bags. Label each bag with the name or letter of the template.

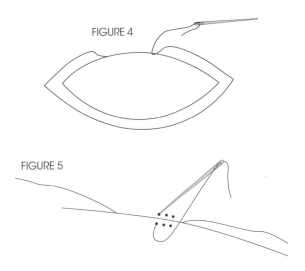

FIGURE 4

FIGURE 5

When working on the inside curves, you will need to clip the seam allowance (*Figures 6 & 7*). If the fabric has been cut on the bias, this may not be necessary.

When stitching a point, stitch to the end and make a second stitch right on the point.

Carefully fold back the appliqué and trim the excess fabric from the back seam allowance (the seam allowance you have already turned under—not from the side yet to stitch) (*Figure 8*).

Continue along the other side of the appliqué shape (*Figure 9*).

When stitching bias stems, sew the concave side first because the convex side will stretch.

The closer the stitches are on tight curves, the smoother the curve will be.

Fussy Cutting

Fussy cutting is the process of cutting a specific area of the design or pattern from a fabric. When cut in multiples and restitched, this method can create lovely patterns and symmetry.

To make a fussy-cut shape, you can use a commercial template cut from acrylic or make your own from template plastic. Just make sure you can see through whatever material you choose as your template.

Use your template as a window to audition your fabrics until you're happy with what you see. Draw a few registration marks on your template to help position your template for the next design. Trace around the edge of the template. This line becomes your cutting line.

Be sure to include a ¼" (6mm) seam allowance all the way around your design, or the finished shape will be smaller than you intend. You can block out the seam allowance with a permanent marker or masking tape. This will give you an exact window for viewing your design while still allowing you to cut in the correct place.

To calculate your fabric requirements when fussy cutting, you'll need to know how many repeats are in the print and how many you will need to complete your design. It's a good idea to take your template with you when you shop for fabrics.

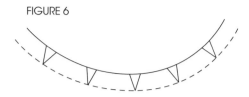

FIGURE 6

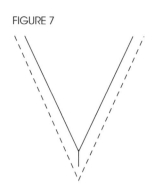

FIGURE 7

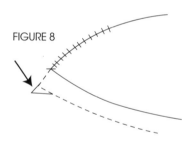

FIGURE 8

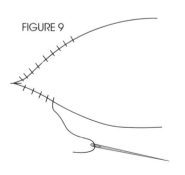

FIGURE 9

Foundation Piecing

Foundation piecing is a great technique to use when you want to make a block with incredibly fine points, curved wedges or some other difficult shape. With this method, there will be less error on difficult designs because you will be sewing on drawn lines.

As the name suggests, you are sewing onto a foundation or base. This base can be paper, fine muslin, freezer paper, preprinted design sheets or products specifically designed for this process, such as Pellon Stitch-N-Tear.

If using plain paper, try to purchase lightweight copy or printer paper (80gsm or less). This will be easier to see through and will also take less effort to remove.

Another benefit to using plain paper or special foundation papers is they can be fed through most photocopiers and printers. This makes it easy to reproduce your piecing guide onto the paper. If using a product like Stitch-N-Tear, you'll need to trace the design onto the sheet by hand.

If using preprinted foundation paper, the seam allowance will most likely be marked, but when tracing your own from a pattern, check to see whether this is included. If not, add the seam allowance to the fabric when trimming around your blocks.

When stitching through the paper, it's a good idea to reduce the stitch length on your machine. More perforations make the paper easier to remove after your piecing is complete.

If you make a mistake, however, the smaller stitches will make it more difficult to rip out your seams. Using a slightly larger needle, such as a size 90/14, will help. This needle needs to be discarded when the foundation piecing is completed because it will be blunt from stitching into the paper.

An open-toe presser foot is helpful when foundation piecing, as it makes the stitching lines easier to see.

Backstitching at the beginning and end of each line prevents your stitches from unravelling during the paper-removal process. A seam ripper is also handy when dealing with stubborn papers.

Lightweight cotton fabrics work well for creating your foundation-pieced design. When pressing them, use a dry iron. Steam can curl the papers.

The positioning of the fabrics on the foundation can be confusing when you begin. Take your time and visualize where the fabric will be when you flip it. After the first few pieces, it'll be smooth sailing.

HOW TO FOUNDATION PIECE

Copy or trace one page for each block or unit that requires foundation piecing.

Position the first fabric on the back side of the foundation with the wrong side of the fabric against the paper. Make sure you have more than the ¼" (6mm) seam allowance extending past the edges.

Place the next fabric against the first with the right sides together. Fold the foundation back on the line and check to be sure you have enough seam allowance. Stitch on the printed line.

Trim the seam allowance if necessary, then flip the fabric and press. Continue across the foundation. Position, check, stitch, trim and press.

Trim when complete. Remember, your final piece of fabric must include at least ¼" (6mm) seam allowance beyond the edge of the paper.

If your pieces are curves, as in *Wheel of Fortune*, stitch around the edge of the paper, but not through the paper, when joining the units together.

Remove the paper, being careful not to disturb the stitches.

> ------------------------------------**NOTE**
> Foundation piecing is sometimes referred to as paper piecing, but I prefer not to use this term because it can be confused with English paper piecing, which is a different technique.

Borders

One of the most valuable things I have learned in quilting is the importance of measuring when adding borders.

Even though a pattern will give you the measurements for cutting borders, your quilt might be just a little different. Your seam allowance might not be as accurate, or the bias edges on the blocks might stretch just a little. You might also decide to add a second or third border to increase the size of your quilt. Use the given measurements as a guide rather than a concrete number when deciding how much fabric to buy or what length to cut your borders.

Some people plan the borders for their quilts at the very beginning, but I usually decide at the end of the piecing process. At this stage, you will have a much clearer picture of what will complement the quilt top. Borders need to add to the overall appeal of the design; they should not look as though they're there only to add extra inches (centimeters).

Auditioning fabrics and deciding the width of the border is extremely important and affects the balance of the quilt. Borders can be narrow or wide, cut from a single fabric, pieced or appliquéed. They can surround individual blocks, part of the quilt or the whole quilt.

By following these suggestions, you will find that your quilt top is placed in an accurate and square frame. It will sit or hang much straighter.

TIP------------------------------------
You might find that either the quilt top or the border is slightly longer than the other. Stitch with this piece closest to the feed dogs of your sewing machine. This will help to evenly distribute the extra length.

MEASURING FOR THE BORDERS

1 | To determine the length of your side borders, measure the length of the quilt at three different locations: the center of the quilt and on either side of the center (*Figure 1*). Never measure down the outermost edges, because these can often stretch and give a false measurement.

2 | Add these three measurements together and divide that total by three. Cut both of your borders to this average measurement.

3 | Fold the border in half to find its midpoint and mark it with a pin. Do the same on the quilt top.

4 | Pin these midpoints, right sides together, and pin at each end.

5 | Ease the border and the quilt top together, pinning at intervals along each side.

6 | Stitch the borders in place using a ¼" (6mm) seam allowance.

7 | Press the seams to one side. You usually want to press the seams toward the borders.

8 | Repeat this process for the top and bottom borders (*Figure 2*).

FIGURE 1

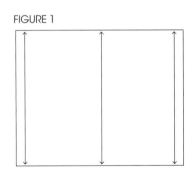

FIGURE 2

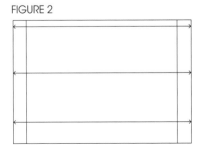

MITERING CORNERS ON A BORDER

If you wish to miter the corners of the border, it's not difficult. Simply follow the instructions below.

1 | Measure your quilt as described in the previous section to determine the average measurement (see Figure 1 and Figure 2 on page 117).

2 | Calculate the border lengths (*Figure 3*).
   For example, if your quilt top measures 62½" (158.8cm) square (including seam allowance), and your border is cut at 5½" (14cm) wide, the length will need to be as follows: 62" (157.5cm) (finished quilt top measurement) + 5" (12.7cm) + 5" (12.7cm)(finished border width on each side) + ½" (1.3cm) (seam allowance) + 3" (7.6cm) extra = 75½" (191.8cm).
   Cut at this length.

3 | Mark your borders at the center mark, then measure half the distance from this measurement in each direction (*Figure 4*). This will center your borders.

4 | Stitch the four borders to the quilt top. **Note:** *You must leave the ¼" (6mm) seam allowance unstitched at each corner on all borders.*

5 | Fold the quilt top on the diagonal, right sides together, to form a 45° angle. Make sure your borders are lined up carefully with the outside edges so they're perfectly straight. The seamlines should sit on top of one another.

6 | Position the edge of your ruler along the fold of your quilt top. The marked 45° angle on the ruler should be aligned with the border seam (*Figure 5*).

7 | Carefully draw a line, remove the ruler, pin to hold borders securely in place and take the quilt to the sewing machine (you may also stitch this by hand if you choose). Lower the needle into the border fabric exactly where the sewing stopped on the border previously: ¼" (6mm) from the edge. This is where the miter will begin. Sew to the edge of the border following the drawn line precisely.

8 | Sew the remaining three corners in the same way.

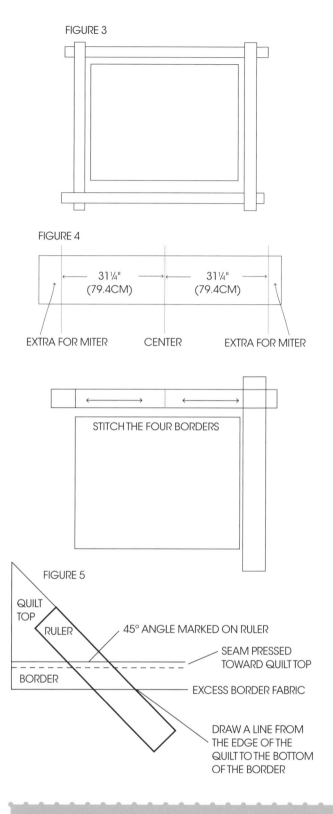

FIGURE 3

FIGURE 4

31¼" (79.4CM)   31¼" (79.4CM)

EXTRA FOR MITER   CENTER   EXTRA FOR MITER

STITCH THE FOUR BORDERS

FIGURE 5

QUILT TOP

RULER

45° ANGLE MARKED ON RULER

SEAM PRESSED TOWARD QUILT TOP

BORDER

EXCESS BORDER FABRIC

DRAW A LINE FROM THE EDGE OF THE QUILT TO THE BOTTOM OF THE BORDER

TIP--
Most quilts will look more balanced if the side borders are stitched first, then the top and bottom borders.

9 | Trim the excess border fabric, leaving a ¼" (6mm) seam allowance. Press the seams of the miter open so they will lie flat, then press all seam allowances away from the quilt body.

Assembly
MAKING THE BACKING
I make my backings from long drops of a single fabric because this reduces the number of seams and makes it easier to hand quilt. Many people, however, like to piece their backings or use multiple fabrics. This is perfectly acceptable and a great way to make a quilt interesting on both sides!

When creating the back, make sure it's about 4" (10.2cm) wider than your quilt on each side. This makes it easier to baste, and you won't have to constantly check to be sure your top isn't extending past the edge of the backing.

If you're sending your quilt to a professional machine quilter, the extra backing fabric is an absolute must. The quilter will require this excess to load the quilt onto the long-arm machine.

When sewing the backing lengths together, remember to remove the selvedges from the fabric first. The selvedge shrinks at a different rate than the rest of the fabric and may cause puckering.

Whether to make your seams vertical or horizontal is a personal preference. I usually make the decision based on the most economical fabric usage.

MARKING THE QUILTING DESIGNS
Marking your chosen quilting design onto your quilt top is usually easiest before you baste the top to the batting and backing.

To mark my quilting lines, I use a 0.7mm mechanical pencil with a 2B lead (or, sometimes, a chalk or ceramic lead) in a color that will be visible on the fabric. It's important to keep your lines fine and light so the lead does not rub deep into your fabric.

Precut stencils can be used to transfer a design to your quilt top, or if you have something in mind, you can make your own stencil from tulle (netting).

Cut the tulle to the size you need. Trace the design onto the tulle with a permanent marker and let it dry. Place the tulle over your quilt and trace the marked lines with your pencil. The design will appear on your quilt as a series of small dots. Like magic!

This method of design transference is extremely versatile, and you can make your design any size you like at the copy center.

If you don't wish to mark your quilt top, quilter's tape (or masking tape) is a great tool. It sticks to the fabric and allows you to use the tape edge as a guide while you quilt. When you're finished, simply peel it off. This tape is especially useful for cross-hatching or Kantha-style quilting.

CHOOSING BATTING
The number of batting choices on the market is huge. When deciding which batting to purchase, you need to consider several things: how thick do you want the batting to be, how warm would you like your quilt to be, how will you wash it, what kind of wear and tear will the quilt get, what price can you afford, what fiber content do you want and what do you want the finished appearance to look like?

The most important decision, however, is how you're going to quilt your quilt. All battings have a specified distance that they must be quilted. For instance, quilt every 3" (7.6cm).

There are recommended quilting distances for both machine quilting and hand quilting. You will achieve much better results if you follow the recommended quilting distance on the batting packaging.

Some batting designed for machine quilting is bonded or contains a scrim, which is a polyester grid that holds the cotton fibers together. These types of batting can be difficult to hand quilt. Batting designed to be hand quilted, however, will not have the stability required for machine quilting. Choose the batting that is appropriate for your style of quilting.

There are battings specifically manufactured to shrink when washed (after your quilting is completed), which causes the fabric to wrinkle around the quilting stitches, giving an antique appearance to the finished project. If this is not the look you want in your finished quilt, look for a batting that will not shrink significantly in the wash.

These are just a few things to consider when deciding what kind of batting to purchase. If you are uncertain, the staff at your local quilt shop should be able to make some recommendations. Many customers at my store like to see and feel the finished quilts, which helps them make a choice.

Remember, your batting should be cut 3–4" (7.6cm × 10.2cm) larger than your quilt top on each side as the batting may move slightly during the quilting process.

Basting

This is the process of making a sandwich from the backing, batting and quilt top.

On a large, flat solid surface such as a table, bench or floor, lay out your prepared backing right-side down. Tape this to the surface. I use 2"-wide (5.1cm) painter's tape (available at hardware stores). The backing needs to be taut but not stretched.

Lay the batting on top, being careful not to move the backing, and smooth it out gently.

Lay the quilt top gently over the batting once again; be careful not to let it drag because this will create wrinkles.

I use size-2 curved safety pins approximately 1½" (3.8cm) long; these need to be good quality and rustproof. Start pinning in the center and pin every 3"–4" (7.6cm–10.2cm), radiating from the center out. Once pinned, roll the excess batting and backing to the front, encasing the edges of the quilt top, and pin. This prevents fraying and retains the seam allowance on the edge of the quilt.

You can thread baste with large tacking stitches or use a basting gun if you wish.

Quilting

I am a passionate hand quilter. I have tried machine quilting and didn't find it to my particular taste, though you may enjoy it. But, when you see the words "quilt as desired" at the end of a project, I would highly recommend giving hand quilting a try.

The first question to ask yourself is, to hoop or not to hoop?

The decision is yours. The most common practice is to use a hoop or frame when hand quilting. This method holds your fabric layers together, and it can make it easier to get an even stitch.

Having said this, I'm a lap quilter, and I do not use a hoop. I let gravity and the weight of the quilt provide the tension that keeps my fabric in place.

With time and practice, you will develop a method that works for you. Every quilter has good ideas and advice, so listen to them all and make use of the tips that suit you. You will eventually adapt these nuggets of wisdom into your own style.

When hand quilting, I use 8- or 12-weight Perle thread. Use whatever thread works best for your style. If you prefer more subtle quilting, thinner hand-quilting threads are available. I simply prefer the look and feel of the Perle threads.

To hand quilt, start by tying a knot at the end of your thread about ½" (1.3cm) from the end. Place the needle into the top of the quilt and bring the tip out at the point where you want to begin stitching. The needle should be between your quilt top and the backing. Do not allow the needle to pierce the backing.

Tug gently until the knot pops through the top. It will bury itself in the batting. Gently rub the hole where the knot went through, and it should disappear.

You will be using a running stitch to quilt, and you will want to try to make even stitches on both the front and back of your quilt.

I'm right-handed, so I place my left hand beneath the quilt and use my index finger to feel when the needle has penetrated all the layers. I wear a thimble on the middle finger of my right hand and a finger stall (or finger cot) on the index finger. The stall acts as a needle grip and reduces the strain on my thumb. Your fingers can become quite tender when you first begin, and the use of aids is helpful.

When your line of running stitches is complete and you've stitched the final stitch, hold your thread and tie a loop knot. Slide the knot down to the quilt surface and tighten close to the fabric.

Insert the needle into the fabric and batting (not the backing) near your last stitch and come back up a short distance away. Pull up and pop the knot into the batting, as you did at the beginning of the thread, then snip the thread close to the top with a pair of small scissors (embroidery scissors are best so you don't accidentally cut your quilt top). The knot and tail should be buried in the batting.

Binding
CREATING THE BINDING

To create your binding, measure each side of your quilt and add the lengths together for a total measurement, then add an extra 12" (30.5cm) to that total. Cut as many strips as needed across the width of your chosen binding fabric to equal this length (remember to consider seam allowances for each strip when cutting).

Overlap your strips at a 90° angle. You will sew at 45° degrees, from corner to corner, within the square created by the overlapped fabric. Trim using a ¼" (6mm) seam allowance. When finished, press the seams open. This will disperse the bulk and make a neater binding.

Fold your binding strip in half lengthwise, wrong-sides together, and press. Align the raw edges of the binding with the raw edge of the quilt on the right side of the quilt. It's best to start your binding on the side of the quilt instead of at a corner, especially if you want to miter your corners.

Leave 6" (15.2cm) of your binding unstitched when you begin. This tail will make it easier to finish the binding at the end.

Pin or use binding clips to hold the binding in place, then machine stitch using a ¼" (6mm) seam allowance. Use a walking foot to minimize drag or stretching of the fabric. (If your machine has a dual feed system, you will not need the walking foot.)

MITERING CORNERS

When you approach a corner, stop stitching ¼" (6mm) before the end. Backstitch to secure the threads and remove the quilt from the machine.

Turn the quilt and prepare to stitch the next side. Fold the binding up to create a 45° angle, then fold it down so the raw edges of the binding and the quilt on the next side are aligned. You should have a fold along the top of the binding at this stage. This fold will sit level with the side of the quilt top already stitched. Start stitching with a ¼" (6mm) seam allowance. Repeat this process for the other corners.

FINISHING THE BINDING

When you have completed all the corners and are approaching your starting point, sew until you have a gap of approximately 12" (30.5cm), including the first 6" (15.2cm) you left unsewn at the beginning of the quilt.

Remove the quilt from the machine. Lay the unsewn binding along the quilt and overlap the binding by the same length as the width the binding was cut (for example, 2½" [6.4cm]). Cut the binding. Open up the folds of the unstitched ends. Place the tails right sides together, overlapping at a 90° angle. Sew at a 45° angle, from corner to corner, inside the square created by the overlap. Check for correct positioning, then trim the seam allowance. Refold and align with the quilt edge. Finish sewing the binding.

Trim the backing and batting to approximately ⅛" (3mm) from the edge of the quilt. This will create a fuller binding.

Fold the binding over the raw edge of the quilt. You can secure this edge with pins or binding clips if you wish, or you may simply fold it with your fingers as you move down the length of the quilt side.

Use a slipstitch to secure the binding to the back of the quilt. The edge of the binding should just cover the line of machine stitching from where you attached the binding to the front of the quilt.

All that's left now is to snuggle up and enjoy your quilt!

RESOURCES

Creative Grids rulers
www.creativegridsusa.com

Aurifil threads
www.aurifil.com

**DMC Perle threads
and Chenille needles**
www.dmc.com

Olfa rotary cutters and mats
www.olfa.com

Clover notions
www.clover-mfg.com

Bernina sewing machines
www.bernina.com

Quilters Dream Batting
www.quiltersdreambatting.com

Karen Kay Buckley Perfect Circles
www.karenkaybuckley.com

**Jeana Kimball straw and
redwork needles**
wwww.jeanakimballquilter.com

**Quilt Treasures
The Quilters Guild Heritage Search**
Kangaroo Press

Roxanne Glue-Baste-It
Available from your local quilt store
or online

Reynolds Freezer Paper
Available from your local quilt store
or grocery store

Template plastic
Available from your local quilt store
or craft retailer

ACKNOWLEDGMENTS

How lucky I am to be part of an amazing community of like-minded women and men. I feel privileged to belong to such a wonderful group and would like to acknowledge the people who, over the years, have nurtured and continued this craft that we now enjoy. There were times when crafting wasn't cool, and without these rebels who stitched on regardless, we might have lost this art. To all of you: thank you, thank you, thank you.

To my present-day supporters, another big thank you.

To my customers and students, I learn so much from you. Without the encouragement and support from you all, I couldn't continue.

To my family, Richard, Meg, Abby and Lucy: I know, at times, the fabric has taken over our lives, but it was always really pretty to look at! Thank you all for just being you. Thank you for keeping me on track and always encouraging me, even when I had just cut the last piece of my favorite fabric incorrectly.

You have, over the years, put up with take-out meals and a lack of ironing (except the quilts) when I needed to get something finished.

You are my everything.

Also, a big thank-you to Lucy, who took over the reins at Amitié Textiles when my husband whisked me off to live in Al Ain in the United Arab Emirates. You have done a stellar job managing everything while being supported by the talented staff and teachers.

Thank you, all.

I know what an incredibly lucky gal I am. I sit at my sewing machine or in my favorite chair hand stitching and remind myself that this career I have is one of privilege and pleasure.

Index

▶ **ABOUT THE AUTHOR.** I have been lucky to have had two wonderful careers. My first love was midwifery, and I was honored to be included in life's most precious everyday miracles.

I tried almost every craft, then, a little over thirty years ago, I stumbled into quilting. Here I have remained. An interest became an obsession, which then became my career.

I would describe myself as a traditional quilter with a modern twist. I love scrappy quilts, and the more fabrics I can use in a single project, the happier I am. In my perfect world, I would hand stitch everything, but with today's busy lifestyle, I do machine piece as well.

Most of my quilts include hand- and machine-piecing, hand-appliqué and hand-quilting methods. Some of my personal favorites, which demonstrate my style, are GREEN TEA AND SWEET BEANS, GYPSY WIFE, STEAMPUNK and THE CIRCLE GAME.

I have owned quilt stores for over fifteen years and currently own Amitié Textiles in Melbourne, Australia (www.amitie.com.au and Instagram @amitie_textiles). The store stocks an eclectic mix of fabrics including Japanese fabrics, Liberty of London, linens from Europe, French toiles and a wide collection of patchwork fabrics. The store offers wonderful service and classes, and hosts local and international tutors.

I currently live in Al Ain, Abu Dhabi, UAE with my husband. I have left the store in the capable hands of Lucy, my youngest daughter, and my experienced staff.

This has enabled me to spend more time expanding and developing patterns under my own label. My days are filled with samples and pattern writing, which is very exciting. To view these, go to jenkingwelldesigns.blogspot.com.

If you would like to follow my progress on designs and daily life, you are most welcome to follow me on Instagram @jenkingwell.

www.fwcommunity.com

19 18 17 16 15   5 4 3 2 1

DISTRIBUTED IN CANADA BY FRASER DIRECT
100 Armstrong Avenue
Georgetown, ON, Canada L7G 5S4
Tel: (905) 877-4411

DISTRIBUTED IN THE U.K. AND EUROPE BY F&W
MEDIA INTERNATIONAL
Brunel House, Newton Abbot, Devon, TQ12 4PU, England
Tel: (+44) 1626 323200, Fax: (+44) 1626 323319
Email: enquiries@fwmedia.com

DISTRIBUTED IN AUSTRALIA BY CAPRICORN LINK
P.O. Box 704, S. Windsor NSW, 2756 Australia
Tel: (02) 4560-1600   Fax: (02) 4577-5288
Email: books@capricornlink.com.au

SRN: T1091
ISBN-13: 978-1-4402-4058-4

Edited by Noel Rivera
Designed and art directed by Brianna Scharstein
Production coordinated by Jennifer Bass
Photography by Al Parrish
Styling by Lauren Siedentopf
Styled photographs shot on location at Heritage Village Museum in Sharonville, Ohio

METRIC CONVERSION CHART		
CONVERT......TO..........MULTIPLY BY		
Inches	Centimeters	2.54
Centimeters	Inches	0.4
Feet	Centimeters	30.5
Centimeters	Feet	0.03
Yards	Meters	0.9
Meters	Yards	1.1

TRY THESE OTHER GREAT QUILT BOOKS!

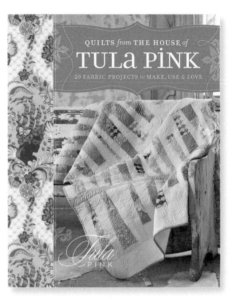

Fresh from the Clothesline
Quilts and Small Projects
by Darlene Zimmerman

For years, quilter, teacher and designer Darlene Zimmerman has been creating exclusive patterns of quilts and small projects for retailers with her Clothesline Club collection. Now, 22 top-drawer quilting and sewing projects are brought to you in *Fresh From The Clothesline*! You'll find a fun range of projects from the quick-to-sew to the large-and-loving-them quilts, all featuring beautiful 1930s reproduction fabrics. A further 6 variations illustrate how to make use of the new fabric designs on the market.

ISBN-13: 978-1-4402-1775-3
SRN: W0937

Quilts from the House of Tula Pink
20 Fabric Projects to Make, Use & Love
by Tula Pink

Welcome to the world of cutting-edge fabric designer Tula Pink, where clever quilts show off fanciful fabric, and your imagination can be let out to play. Featuring fabrics that you know and love, Tula offers 20 patterns with her signature flair for color, design and original style. Between 10 amazing quilts and 10 extra-cool companion projects, you'll be inspired to play with fabric, color and design like never before!

ISBN-13: 978-1-4402-1818-7
SRN: W1582